Seasons of Sonship Foundations Book 1

Joshua F. Todd

DEDICATION

This series is dedicated to my parents, both natural and spiritual, who have helped me find Jesus.   It is dedicated to my brothers who have walked with me. It is dedicated to sons and daughters who have helped expand me. It is dedicated to my loving wife and children who have filled me.

CONTENTS

ACKNOWLEDGMENTS

Just recently, one of the clearest voices for kingdom leadership in America said that fathering is the most critical issue of our times. I have been writing, teaching, preaching, leading, discipling, and practicing fathering for decades with the emphasis upon "this is what we will need as we approach the 2020's." I have written books on the subject, and I have taught CORE classes in our Kingdom Leadership Institute with this emphasis. I have also teamed up with Joshua Todd to teach about fathering, with his part of the teaching focused upon "how to be fathered." His part was received with greater enthusiasm than mine.

I can speak to the authenticity of this book: Joshua Todd is the real deal. We have walked together through "some stuff" for more than a decade. What he writes is real life, on target, and as crucial to your personal spiritual life as it can be. Fathering begins with the Father. So does everything else. All Creation exists because He wants it. All Creation answers to the fathering heart. Father has a Son bringing many sons into Glory.

Nothing the enemy of your eternal purpose has ever done to you can damage your destiny more than unhealed issues with fathering leaders. Nothing clarifies your submission to Father like your submission to fathering leaders. Nothing opens the way for Father's highest in your life than the way you honor fathers of flesh and spirit. So, reading this book may challenge the most basic building blocks upon which you developed your present point of view and trust levels that measure your relationships. Reading this book may be the significant next step in your spiritual walk that prepares and positions you for the fulfillment of your personal purpose.

To best answer the question, "Who should write this book?" I would offer this insight: This book should be written by someone with more than theories about fathering or reporting what they can summarize from research. This book should be the overflow of experience tested by fathering familiarity and failures. It should be written by someone with level of expertise in apostolic and prophetic function since the fathering spirit matures those foundations. Joshua Todd is the person to write this book. No one has anticipated it more than I have. I am confident it will influence and impact many lives. It has all the markings of a classic. I am proud of this man of God in all the right ways. Thank you, Joshua, for living this life and communicating this truth. - Dr. Don Lynch

FINALLY, IT'S HERE!! I have felt for some time now we were going to enter a moment where some of the best songs, sermons, and books of our lifetime were about to emerge and come on the scene. Then in walks such a young man into my life. The first time I met Joshua Todd, I knew I had just encountered a young man who didn't only speak a word, but he had lived a word.

As I have grown to know Joshua personally, I have found out that it's not about "stage presence" that makes him unique but instead backstage pass, behind the scene look at the life he has lived when you open this book that's exactly what you're getting. You are about to pull the curtain back and see what happens and needs to happen to prepare you for the stage God has meant for you to stand on. What you will not find in this book is a fast-paced, hurry up and write something trendy and fast, or something clever and crafty but instead, you will find a quality that's not written by a pen but something that's been scribed on the heart of a son. I believe "Seasons of Sonship" is a right on time book that could not be written until now. Several books have written on this topic and have been helpful, but many come based on what was happening presently, but as you turn the pages of this book, you will find that God has had true sons walking out the seasons of sons for many unseen years. You will find many times that those who make it out of the gate first are not the same as those who finish the race. I believe books like this cannot be written out before they are lived out, and Joshua Todd is such a son as this. As you begin to turn the pages of this book, I believe it will also begin to "turn the heart of sons toward the fathers" with clarity and with power and understanding. I can see many Fathers & Sons together going through the pages of this book together as they go through the "Seasons of Sonship." ENJOY & ENGAGE.
-David Kelly, The Freedom Center, Paducah, KY

Everywhere we look, there seems to be an ever-increasing need for fathers. Even the world, in their lack of understanding, cries out for them. The Lord has been faithful, and he has raised up fathers who are stepping up to receive and train up sons. As I look around me, I see an army of them. Like Jesus, many of these fathers are unassuming and unrecognized, and they carry, within themselves, treasures of great value to be inherited and passed on to future generations.

So many fathers, like the Heavenly Father, himself, are standing with arms wide open to receive their sons, but the Church has forgotten how to be sons. Most of us are running around like prodigals, searching for our true identity and purpose, bemoaning the traumatic things that have happened to us(beginning with the failures of our natural born parents), and placing unrealistic and inappropriate expectations on the fathers who step up. In our rebellion, it is hard to see that we are pushing away the very thing we need, and we reject the fathering that is offered to us.

Before I took Apostle Josh's class on Sonship, I thought I lacked nothing as a spiritual daughter, and because of the tendency to "compare ourselves by ourselves," I thought I was doing great. However, the wisdom released into my life through the birthing of this revelation of Holy Spirit, through a beautifully and uncommonly surrendered vessel, has opened my eyes to see the ways I have placed limitations on my relationship with spiritual father by my own wounds and lack of knowledge in this area. I did not know that I needed to learn to be a daughter.

Over the years, I have been witness as my friend, turned brother, and eventually, a spiritual father, has grown and emerged from preacher, to prophet, to apostle. The keys he has shared in this book and in the series that will follow uncovers revelation that I have personally witnessed Apostle Josh walking out in his own life for over 15 years. This work highlights the shared failures, pitfalls, and limitations to be overcome by sons who wish to receive what God wants to release to us and through us.

We have a responsibility to allow Father, through our spiritual fathers, to shape and mature us into sons and daughters who have the character, endurance, and strength of will to carry on the inheritance he has entrusted to our spiritual fathers. This book is step one. I encourage you not to stop here, but to step up to the challenge of eating and digesting this steak, piece by piece, and allow it to become a part of your spiritual DNA. I believe it will change your life and the lives of the generations after you.

-Melody Bolduc, CEO
Keys Educational Resource Center

In Kingdom culture there is perhaps no more critical dynamic to grasp than that between the Father and Son. In this relationship can be found the definition and initiation of everything that is converging to fulfill the purposes of God in the earth. Within Joshua's words you can hear the sound of the Father expressed through his authentic sonship. As you read you will discover a practical and strategic roadmap for the journey into sonship that will not only set you on the right path through fathering leadership, but will prepare you to avoid the pitfalls in the road. At great cost, Joshua has pioneered sonship through submission and obedience and with great vulnerability of personal experience he lays out a vision that is both clear and powerful.

I challenge everyone to take this book to heart – prayerfully, intentionally – and allow this message to grip you, as it has me. Embrace the journey marked out in these pages, endure the process to be prepared, and surrender to the Father's purpose as you navigate through your own seasons of sonship.

-Sean D. Harvey, author of Formed in Secret and Culture of Sonship

In a generation where fatherlessness has become an epidemic that threatens the emergence of strong new leaders, Joshua offers the cure by issuing the call for sons to turn their hearts back toward fathers. The history of humanity has built into its foundation, a culture of legacy, inheritance, endurance, and growth through fathering relationships. Since the inception of tribes and nations, there have always been fathers that have provided wisdom, strategy, encouragement, and discipleship to inspire sons from potential into the ultimate expression of purpose.

The nation of Israel had the patriarchs like Abraham, Isaac, and Jacob; the early church had patristic fathers like Ignatius of Antioch to John of Damascus; America had its founding fathers from George Washington to Benjamin Franklin. God began the story of man by introducing himself as a father, desiring that we relate to Him in this way, first and foremost. In the gospels, we see that Jesus was defined as the son of God and He was the ultimate son who inherited all that was the Father's, providing for us the ultimate example of what sonship can become.

In Seasons of Sonship, Joshua writes from the viewpoint of a son, but with the wisdom of a Father. The stories, principles, and revelation that he reveals within its pages have come from many years of personally walking out its realities. When I consider those, who are the most qualified to speak about spiritual fathering and sonship, Joshua Todd is a pristine example and a powerful voice calling everyone who reads this book into essential fathering relationships. Joshua is the picture of what it looks like to be fathered well, because he has been fathered well and is now inspired to write about it. The point of this book is help sons properly relate and receive from the essential fathering relationships that God the father is bringing into their lives. This requires humility, trust, and submission for which this book carefully lays a foundation. May many powerful and thoroughly equipped sons emerge within this generation and beyond as a fruit of reading this book. May they continue to grow into new seasons of spiritual fatherhood that bring forth new generations of sons!

-Derek Kirkman

MY SONSHIP STORY

It was April 1993. I was out of breath, locked in my room, heart pounding within my ears as I had barely escaped the thugs that had chased me home that day. This was my life. I was depressed in every sense of the word. My life looked like someone who was in crisis. I was miserable on the inside.

That day in April, I cleaned my room and prepared my "note." I went into the restroom to hang myself. As I stood on the toilet I thought, how interesting that this is the last thing I would see before died. In my religious upbringing suicide meant you would always end up in hell no matter what. That is how bad I was on the inside.

The front door opened, and I heard my mom come home early from work. I abandoned my selfish notion and hastily retreated. As I sat in my room, sweating profusely, she came in and told me to get dressed and that I was going to a church event. I remember thinking, "I will just hang myself when it's over," and that was what I intended to do.

At the church, a young Evangelist began to preach about this God-man Jesus whose life, death, and resurrecton changed everything. The message gripped me, and waves of conviction, love, and hope washed over me powerfully as I succumbed to it. A group of adults had to carry me out before the altar call because I was weeping loudly with the conviction that God wanted me. That night, the Lord spoke to me for the first time and made it clear that I belonged to Him and that truth would impact every decision I made after that night. I stopped living "my life" just the same as if I had committed suicide; instead, my life was going to be used for a higher purpose.

The call into ministry came a few years later in 1996, when I was only 16. I immediately began to pursue ministry as my future. As soon as I could drive, I was going to every church function, Bible Study, and discipleship group I could find, all of the Southern Baptist variety. I was driving out to the middle of nowhere to my favorite place to pray and staying out all night worshipping the Lord. I was asking questions that would stump the teachers, and yet, the wounds of my youth were open doors into my life.

I struggled with profound rejection, fear, and sexual sin that consistently ran through my mind. As most good Southern Baptists would do in this case, I memorized scripture, writing it on my heart so that I would not sin against God as King David had said to do in Psalms. The sin continued driving my pursuit to be free, and the harder I ran, the faster it seemed to become. The temperature of my life was lukewarm. Though I had a zeal for God and a desire to be used, I was failing morally.

The Word Of The Lord

In 1998, I knew the call of God was on my life and that I should attend Christian University, but instead I accepted a music scholarship to the University of North Florida's Jazz program. Music was my escape for much of my life. It was the best program in the nation at the time and was too tempting to pass up. The voice of God was still all over me, however, to pursue the call on my life. I accepted the scholarship but Jesus followed me there.

A year into the program, I was practicing music 8 hours a day, and yet my musical ability was declining. I couldn't explain it! I did the right things: listened to other musicians for hours, studied theory, and practiced; yet still, It was undeniable that something very important was missing. Finally, the director of the program called me into his office to talk. It was the most humbling experience of my life, but I couldn't disagree with him that I was indeed getting much worse the harder I tried!

I wished it weren't true but there no more denying it. Suddenly, right in the middle of him speaking, I had my first supernatural encounter. Time froze. His hand was extended, his mouth left half opened in mid-sentence, staring. I looked around His office and everything was as he was. Out of nowhere, a deep and powerful voice sounded over me, the love and acceptance and sheer power touched every cell. The question was simple, but each word was a container of something at a grander scale. "How long will you run from the call on your life?"

As soon as I received the question within myself, time caught up, and the next sentence that came out of his mouth was confirmation. "It just seems like there is something more important to you." I merely nodded my head and handed over my entire music folder. Though he tried to talk me out of it, I resigned and forfeited my scholarship and received F's in all of the remaining classes for that semester. I asked the Lord as I walked off the school campus that day to show me that I was obedient and, knowing what I would walk through at home having made such a hasty decision, to give me mercy.

Next thing I know, my phone was vibrating in my pocket, and it was my Pastor at the time. He had spoken with someone who had told him that I had a call on my life, and he offered me the position of Student Pastor. By the time I reached my car that day, I was "in ministry," and God showed up miraculously. For the next year, we watched the hand of God move across our students.

The group outgrew every place they put us, kids were sharing their faith, and we saw kids converted off the streets who are serving the Lord in nations to this day. Things were going well! I was now fully convinced the hand of God was on my life, yet the wounds of rejection, abandonment, fear and sexual sin followed me around. I saw the move of God in my novice as if it meant God was overlooking my obvious moral failures. He wasn't.

To Passion-Land | 2000

Now I was back with my parents. I remember waking up one day with a large nodule on my neck right above my lymph node. It was very sore and I was fatigued but I tried to ignore it until the mass grew to the size of a small orange. Finally, full of fear, I went to the family doctor, who showed great concern. After the first tests, the doctor and his assistant stepped outside leaving the door cracked. I heard him say to his assistant, "I think this is non-Hodgkin's Lymphoma, and we need to admit him for tests."

I instantly felt the blood leave my face and blame towards God in my heart. I finally had the evidence my wounded soul had been looking for that God wasn't good to me while I had seen Him be good to others through my ministry. I went home and tried to hide the concern from my parents to no avail. I was too weak even to argue or share detail. I just went to my room to sleep and pray. The voice of God came crashing into my room that night and said that He desired me to go to travel with a team of musicians that had tried to recruit me into evangelistic campaigns the year before. I responded with a sarcastic question. "Maybe you didn't hear the news, Lord, but they say I may have cancer, so now may not be the best time to go." He responded quickly, "Go, and I will heal you."

I responded that if, indeed, He healed me, I would go. The next morning, I awoke, and the mass was completely gone. Of course, I thanked the Lord for His healing power, but I never made the call to the missionary group. A few days later, I awoke, and the mass was back. I went before the Lord in deep sorrow and repented. I called the team and told them I would fly out to their training camp in California If they still wanted me. I officially became part of the interdenominational ministry group, and the next day the mass was gone and has never returned. The group told me my missionary budget of $4,000 was due in 5 days. I had just been healed, and believed God would provide.

My church had seen God's hand on me and even though they were not open to the moving of Holy Spirit, it was apparent God was on my life. My pastor at the time wanted to help me with $500. He planned to have me come up in front of the church, have me say a few words about the need and then the church would let me stand in the back, and people could come and give me funds as they felt led. When I finished speaking, the Pastor was encouraging me to sit down when a young man stood up in the back.

By this time, the youth had grown from the 4 I had started with to over 120. It wasn't just numbers; it was passion and discipleship. This man had witnessed it very carefully and been impacted by it himself. He spoke out above the crowd of about 200 and said that they had been watching how diligent my leadership was with the youth and how I had been operating on a meager salary, $250 a week at the time. He felt the church should invest and cover my trip to the nations completely.

The blood left my Pastor's face. He stammered and then responded that it would take a unanimous vote for the church to spend that much money from the budget with such short notice. One-by-one, 200 people stood up and applauded, and every cent that I needed for the nations was secured in less than five minutes. I only had a week to prepare, but I was on my way!

Succumbing to the Spirit

The team ended up traveling across the nation, and then an urgent need arose, changing our final destination from Costa Rica to Ireland. We flew to the land of Ireland to minister in Catholic environments and shared the gospel of Jesus Christ. I saw wonderful things! My favorite memory was the time I ministered to IRA (Irish Republican Army) recruits. They were supposed to have been off to terror training camp the next day but said they were no longer interested after getting saved that day!

There was one person on the team that baffled me. She carried such a significant "presence" and such joy that it, frankly agitated me. I loved her, but my mind was at war. Looking back, I was being wooed by Holy Spirit and didn't even know it. One day I finally came to her and asked what It was. Her response to me went against everything I had learned. Southern Baptists mostly believed that Holy Spirit's operation had ceased when the last Apostle died or when the Canon was completed and that is what I had been taught my entire life. Because of this, much of my thinking had been more dispensational on the topic.

I believed the Holy Spirit had a role, but it was to illuminate scripture within the believer, to convict sinners, and that was about it. I did not believe in a "2nd baptism" of the Holy Spirit, exactly what my friend "Mo" had just said I needed. I was at war in my mind but realized something was missing from my life. I wasn't victorious, even though I had seen great things, my life was not holy, not honorable, and not humble. I was hungry, and it saved me.

Even though I didn't mentally agree with her Theology on the subject, I yielded to her, and she prayed for me while that power fell upon me in the middle of Ireland. I succumbed to Holy Spirit. In those days Everything changed after I met Mo. I went back to the Southern Baptist Church, but Holy Spirit moved through me which caused "issues." People got healed, and so more and more people began approaching me for healing prayer. It was getting out of hand. I went and learned under my first true spiritual father, Pastor Peter Young of Victory Center Church. Pastor Peter spent six months teaching me, pouring into me, loving me and showing me the power of God as He released miracles into the lives of hurting people. Never before or since have I seen a man be able to move in such grace and wield "rest" as a weapon.

I encountered so many things in those days: inner healing and deliverance, radical worship, dance, and more! It was like I was put into a cocoon, and yet, my wounds and open doors followed me. I would do well, and then my sin would steal my peace, which touched my relationships. In my prayer time, it was more begging God to deliver me so I didn't have to live a double standard, and yet, that is what I did during those years. The wounds were still there.

When I came back to my hometown of Jacksonville, everything was different. My old church found out about my actions in moving with the Holy Spirit and had an "intervention." I left that church and began to save and work to pay for seminary, which I attended for two years until my spirit man was close to death. I went to work at another Baptist church as an interim Pastor, but miracles began to break out, and well-meaning deacons sought to install me permanently against the desire of the Senior Pastor. Rather than be divisive, I resigned the position immediately.

Around this time, I met my wife. I knew instantly she was my wife so-much-so that I proposed on the 2nd date. This would not normally be advisable but then again, we are about to celebrate 12 years of happy marriage, so perhaps it is. We have two beautiful children. Before we met our current spiritual fathering leaders Dr. Don and Ruthanne Lynch, we served a mega-church in town. The church was budding at around 3,000 people who were drawn primarily to the Teacher's charisma and vision for the church. My wife and I attended ministry and pastoral school at this church.

Interrupted

When the long-awaited time came for us to go on staff, God interrupted again, and set our hearts in motion to connect with Dr. Don. We didn't know why at the time, but today, that ministry no longer exists. One day, my wife brought home a pamphlet for a local ministry that seemed missional, and it struck a chord deep in my heart. I knew we had to go.

This church was unlike anything we had ever seen. The leader was strong, speaking with an authoritative tone. The truth that was being released was touching places deep within us both. I was paying close attention, looking for warning signs, when that same booming voice of the Lord came all around me declaring, "This is your spiritual father."

That was over ten years ago. Immediately, the fathering relationship that God had assigned began to prove itself as the "thing I was missing."

What I had learned in Ireland of hunger, and the mega-church of honor had prepared me to learn humility and holiness and introduced me to a time of walking out some of the fundamental concepts of this book. I have been pregnant with this revelation for the last twelve years, and the baby has been forming for this time. Through my fathering relationship with Dr. Don, I have walked through prophetic and apostolic preparation, gleaned eldership expertise, and learned to represent him and Jesus in nations of the earth. Most importantly, I have been set free from the sin that so easily entangled me and no longer live a life of compromise.

My marriage is healthy. My finances are healthy. My family is stable and secure. I am a finisher, whereas I never finished anything before. I justified quitting, ditching, vagabonding, and the like with overly-spiritual avoidance. Now, what I begin, I finish.

This book, Seasons of Sonship, Foundations, the first of the series, will provide you with some key concepts to progress in sonship stature, by becoming secure in your sonship submission. You won't have to read another book in this series to learn what is needed to advance as a son. The five "season" books will exist to help guide you in and out of each season.

The five seasons I have examined in sonship are Invitation, Interdependence, then to the Interchange, on to Invocation and finally into <u>Inheritance</u> will be texts that help you navigate the norms of these distinctively different "seasons."

Some definitions

A son is simply a kingdom citizen that can progress in stature to the place of being an heir and a fathering leader. When the Bible speaks of sons in the New Testament understanding of inheritance, it always includes women. Women make some of the greatest "sons" and at various times and reasons, the term "daughter" will be mentioned but for the sake of the material is always assumed. In the Kingdom fathers and sons are men and women. Think of "son" as a standing with a corresponding function, not a gender. We could say ,"heirs", "sons" or "daughters" the reality is that all of these labels speak back those being prepared to inherit and represented Jesus, the greatest Fathering leader.

The word **seasons**, which is used across the prophetic arena as a general way of saying "expect something different," is not in this sonship series used solely in the sense of timing, but also in the sense of temperature, environment, and foliage. These descriptors will be expounded upon later in much greater detail. In the seasons of sonship, these "environments" have corresponding processes, protocols, and promises.

These different seasons also have "sounds" much like an infant knows only how to communicate with a coo. There will not always be distinctive markers between each season, but there will be markers in maturity, tests taken in training, and advances made in the enduring which will prepare the son to enter the next season. It is entirely possible sons can distinguish where they are in the seasons of sonship and prepare to gather the correct things that should be carried, dress themselves in what should be worn, and walk in the paths that should be taken. Misinterpreting a season will leave the son in danger of welcoming what should be rejected while the proper understanding of whereabouts, and what is to be taken, can empower a more excellent and more accelerated sonship progression.

Sonship progression speaks of the consistent movement towards a more advanced state. Sonship moves towards fathering, as the ultimate goal of all sonship is that sons become fathers. It may appear paradoxical, but it is quite essential in the kingdom that all fathers are sons, and all sons become fathers. It is also important in the Kingdom that sons progress towards being heirs, as only heirs inherit! The march towards inheritance should always be in the minds of sons.

Understand **inheritance** as the purpose and the provision required for it to manifest. As every good and perfect gift of the Father comes because of His goodness, everything that comes from the father arrives as inheritance which a son should be prepared to steward into expansion. This truth means that Fathering in the Kingdom is aimed at preparing sons to be heirs, so God's purpose and provision can manifest in the earth. The lack of provision in the church can be understood by a weak grasp of her true purpose. We have 20% of the provision because we are only aware of 20% of the true purpose.

Sonship stature speaks of the authority of the son as evidenced in the process by achievement and ability. Within each of the seasons will come greater progress as a byproduct of that ability. These are not the gifts of the Holy Spirit working through the son. Gifts of Holy Spirit are never a marker of maturity in the son's experience. Holy Spirit has fruit, and the son has "fruit," and therefore requires pruning. The gifts of Holy Spirit flow out of the relationship with Holy Spirit, but as the story above indicates, that is not always consistent with a son's maturity but may be a measurement of a son's pursuit.

Sonship Submission is defined as the level the son must place himself at the disposal of the God-assigned fathering leader for the son to mature, progress, and grow in stature towards heirship, being ready to receive his spiritual inheritance and expand it to the coming generation. The next chapter will discuss the "how-to" of sonship submission.

Fathering leaders can be defined as leaders assigned by God to receive and release the fathering nature of God and the leadership of Jesus in areas of revelation and strategy so that God's nature and purpose are manifested in people, places, and times in accordance with delegated authority. The things that are important about this definition are the words: assigned, heart, purpose, and authority. With any of these things missing, the Fathering relationship is incomplete. The way God desires to release His heart to you is through an imperfect fathering leader who is led by God's Holy Spirit. If you doubt this is Biblical, please take a moment to read "Fathering, Transforming individuals and nations" by Dr. Don Lynch as I will not take time to prove this biblical reality as that has already been done.

The purpose of this book is for those who believe they are sons to embrace the process of becoming mature to the point they can carry a voice within themselves more significant than their own. This is a powerful sonship reality. When the son discovers that his voice has not yet been fully developed, he can allow it to be developed by God's leader to far exceed his current expectation. There are strategies that empower this reality. Today, many son's spend their lives speaking only half of the "volume" God intended because they never learned the secret of carrying someone else's voice bigger than their own. More to come on this in the <u>Season of Interdependence</u>.

But mark this: There will be terrible times in the last days. People will be lovers of themselves, lovers of money, boastful, proud, abusive, disobedient to their parents, ungrateful, unholy, without love, unforgiving, slanderous, without self-control, brutal, not lovers of the good, treacherous, rash, conceited, lovers of pleasure rather than lovers of God—
2 Timothy 3:1-4

Secular culture works against fathering relationships and openly encourages rebellion in an attempt to influence the church against the kind of submission that produces the ultimate of obedience that would transform the culture! People struggle to submit to Fathers and therefore never learn to submit to God to the degree needed for real transformation to occur both in them and through them. A general "uneasiness" falls upon the masses' ears when such terms like submission and obedience are used, but it would be a challenging thing to understand any of the Scriptures with a proper hermeneutic without the foundation stones of submission and obedience.

Just like a building has support beams, sonship has pillars so that the structure which glorifies God is erected. If one or more of these pillars becomes unsteady, the entire structure and stature of the son are at risk. The pillars mentioned within the four strategic areas are a way that Kingdom culture is appropriated into a son's relationship with a fathering leader. Just like Kingdom Culture presents a place where God can stay a while, pillars of sonship present a place where the fitted father and the shaped son can experience the robust transfer of the connection.

This book, is the legend that is a part of a series on sonship that will provide a reference for the future writings that will attempt to walk sons through a process more rapidly than without it. I shared the stories at the beginning to dispel the idea that there will be insurmountable obstacles as this is not true. Just like most reference documents, it will be hard hitting points of reference whereas the corresponding materials will be fuller messaging that are filled with hope and walk sons into loving the process and much as the outcomes. The love and patience in the process is one of the greatest measurements for a ready fathering leader today.

If you think you are the least qualified for sonship, you will most likely make some fathering leader very honored to walk with you. The need for accelerated maturity on sons is upon the church.

1 THE PILLAR OF PURSUIT

Blessed are those who hunger and thirst for righteousness, for they will be filled. -Matthew 5:6

The pillar of pursuit is the pillar that ensures the son will progress and is the place where sonship begins. If the disciple is not following, the master cannot teach. None of the other pillars or areas of submission can be realized unless the son is willing to make the pursuit of his fathering leader a priority. This is how kingdom hunger can be understood, "Blessed are the those that hunger and thirst." The filling comes as a result of finishing a pursuit. In many ways, the pursuit of a son is just that, emptying with the goal of filling up with different things.

Many sons are shocked at what must be emptied to make room to fill while fathers rejoice in the response to revelation that releases greater levels of identity-understanding. Letting go of things that children carry is a marker of spiritual manhood as Paul made clear in discussing the, "when I was as a child" truth, in his fathering letter to the Corinthians. There are strategically "marked moments" of spiritual manhood progression out of being a child, and "emptying" is one of them. This can be understood as "learning to go hungry" that Paul shares later as he discusses contentment.

As the fathering leader is pursued by the son, who has become fixated upon whom the fathering leader represents, opportunities will arise for things within the son's life to come under scrutiny to ensure the proper value is given. A son who believes he is called to be a worship leader because his mother told him so and spends 40 years pursuing that can face the harsh reality that though it existed in the mind of his mother, it never existed in the heart of God for his life. Tragic! This is why discipling that has been left out in the cold needs to become normal again. Discipling is a kingdom norm, and the heart of discipling is fathering leadership. We will speak on this when discussing the pillar of purpose.

A spiritual fathering leader prioritizes purpose with a higher God-granted perspective while the son prioritizes the pursuit and mastering the proper posture. It is quite possible that sons come into the relationship with a fathering leader focused on a false or incomplete purpose since that comes out of the humanism found in many of today's mainstream churches. It is not safe for that son to determine the pursuit's objective at any level. Sons tend to waste; fathers work to build something that will last. Pursuing a false or incomplete purpose leads to wasted time, wasted resources, and eventually, wasted purpose. This is why sons who have no fathering leader many times have a story filled with tremendous waste that matches their tremendous idealism.

While the idea, to some, seems ridiculous- that a son may find a fathering leader after 20 years of ministry experience and be expected to scrap the best of their purpose-pursuit, fathers have a passion that burn against waste and a perspective that gives them the ability to know the difference between waste and "wealth." It is more loving for these fathers to put an end to the waste game and set sons on a journey towards divine purpose sooner rather than later. This journey is filled with grace and glory, the other with only glimpses of grandeur.

Sons who work to convince fathering leaders that they have a good handle on purpose will unknowingly work to have fathers abandon a heavenly perspective. In other words, "salesman sons" who spend time, energy, resources, etc. working to correct their father's perspectives are simply desiring to continue down the way of waste. Fathers are stubborn for a son's sake. It is the job of the fathering leader to identify the hidden purpose, and the job of the son to abandon his own understanding and pursue the fathering leader and the one they represent.

Realize that the son would be pursuing the incorrect purpose in their own strength as God refuses to invest grace as supernatural ability into misguided fantasy. The Fathering leader is agreeing with God by refusing the son's attempt o create an agreement without God and His purpose in the center. Sons often work to get the father to agree with them, while the Father works to get all to agree with God. Big difference!

The minute the fathering leader allows the son to persuade him into an agreement where God and the purpose are not central, the son has become the leader, and the father has unknowingly allowed the roles to be redefined. The son has become the leader and the father ,the follower. Sons cannot lead fathers into inheritance because they cannot take someone somewhere they have never been themselves.

Salesman Sons

Often out of a humanistic and potential-driven system orphans emerge with heart wounds that have been unsuccessfully healed. Though unhealed wounds are illegal in Jesus' kingdom, without the leadership strategy in place (as depicted when Jesus bestowed His gifts upon the church functioning with a fathering heart) untreated wounds abound.

Often these sons with hurt hearts have masterful mouths, and mature fathering leaders know this by the way in which the sons sell their self-images. They often, "think of themselves more highly than they ought," and steer the conversation away from the wreckage and towards some temporary triumph.

These "salesman" sons can be typically spotted as their internal crisis manifest five symptoms:

1. **They almost always end their thought with a question whether spoken or inferred.** An Orphan cannot feel valued and, therefore, constantly needs validation, working to fill a hole within themselves. They will misunderstand the role of a fathering leader to be a continuous voice of validation. Since, often, they have been celebrated in cultures when performing consistently with the culture's objective,

they exhaust themselves doing just that. Orphans do not understand value tied to a premeditated decision by a God, who is love versus performance.

2. **They aren't ready for correction, so they sell a scenario that doesn't require it, often unknowingly.** This scenario sounds great to the untrained spirit, but it is how they perceive reality, not what reality actually is. They need "buy-in" for this scenario to foster an agreement around the false. They often talk continuously to keep from having to listen. This is a fear based relational dynamic and cannot exist if the proper fear will enter this relationship as discussed in Book 3, <u>The Season of Interdependence.</u>

3. **They probe to see if they can find what their leader likes to hear and then serve them that.** This is often tied to the salesman son learning that if they can find the right buttons, they can say the right things. If they can flatter the father into a false agreement, the leader will take the bait; hook, line, and sinker. By this, the salesman son will get to write the fathering story. A fathering story the son writes is not a fathering story at all. As long as this goes on, the son maintains his own "end" in mind. He isn't functioning like a son at all.

4. **They want to create a valuation of themselves outside of reality.** Many of these sons have lived a life that has many high points to share and low points that need to be hidden. They may sell their overall giftedness, wealth, or charisma, but they are desiring that certain subjects stay off the table for discussion. This is control. They want to paint a picture their leader will appreciate rather than give away the whole thing the leader may confiscate. The father will not buy-in to their valuation because fathering leaders have learned to value what God values and dismiss what He ignores.

5. **They often focus more on anointing than character.**

Rather than allowing issues of character to arise, they may focus in on the anointing. This is a mistake right away in discussion with a mature, healthy, fathering leader who realizes anointing has nothing to do with the son at all; rather it is what on the son's life to impact others. When the fathering leader does not celebrate how anointed a son is, the ugly heart issues will surface in the son since that is what the son uses to stroke his weaknesses to sleep.

Priorities

The son, just as mentioned above, has spent much of his life prioritizing based upon his notion of purpose which is usually potential. The father won't buy in. The father will not also pursue the son. "How unloving!" many think, but the opposite is true. The father, who has matured in this process, realizes how tragic it is for the son to waste, but the roles that God defined ensures the power God has made available is accessible.

Because Fathering is spiritually occurring within a natural relational dynamic, there is spiritual power made available. This is why a large part of the fathering role is dealing with grace inhibitors. These pillars of sonship progression that the son masters ensure that all the grace required is released to both parties. Otherwise, waste and wreckage can occur. Whoever is being pursued is greatest in the relationship. This is how hunger works. Hunger empowers believers to worship Jesus. Jesus can measure hunger by worship, often a chilling thought to worship leaders everywhere.

By his pursuit, the son is agreeing that his fathering leader is greater in the relationship. Agreeing with who? God. This means that whoever is being pursued is greater, and he who is pursuing is less. This may seem uncomfortable to think about, but more will be discussed in Chapter two, the pillar of posture, that should settle why one is greater and viewed that way by God, and one is less as the paces of the posture comes into light.

The prioritization aspect of pursuit answers to the basic question: how much can be pursued with excellence? What must be left behind to pursue? How much of this pursuit is performance? Fathers do not expect performance; they measure obedience. Obedience is what God uses to measure, and mature and healthy fathering leaders look for obedience to God, not even obedience to them as a maturity measuring stick.

Order

As long as the son pursues, the relationship is in order. This order produces rest and peace because it requires submission. The pursuit can take many forms but always produces rest and peace. Sons don't strive. If selfish ambition is removed striving becomes pointless. The pursuit does actually brings ambition into focus while teaching endurance. Sons can start but fathers finish, and the pillar of pursuit ensures that throughout each season, the son is learning to run after something they are unable to fully grab hold of. This is healthy!

This is not to say that the pursuit will always feel peaceful and restful. Sometimes this pursuit will require the son to wrestle within themselves. Sometimes the son will fight, stagger, drag themselves, cry, and push into this pursuit. This will purify the pursuit. The greater the pursuit is purified towards purpose the greater the father will celebrate it. This is why many believe fathering leaders to be self-serving when they are actually God-honoring. They are celebrating the pursuit that is now shared not because it means anything for them personally.

The pursuit can be measured as hunger for the completion of the assignment and the receiving of the shared inheritance that the son can learn to expand to future generations. The son is learning to serve the inheritance that is a portion of Jesus' inheritance which can be understood as the assignment. The inheritor is learning, often for the first time, that he/she is not a quitter!

Finding The Finisher

Jesus has the name above all names because He finished His task. I never knew what that felt like in my 20's. That decade consisted of a lot of starting things but never finishing. I started businesses; they failed. I started relationships; they failed until I met my wife at 26. I got great ideas but they never materialized. I went to Seminary and quit. I had friends and failed them. I never finished.

I remember, one day, my fathering leader looked at me and asked if I was going to join the ministry school. I hesitated, knowing that I had been through a combined total of 6 years in ministry school and seminary. He pressed the matter until I reluctantly agreed. It took me 3 years to finish my Bachelors of Practical Ministry, but it marked me forever. I had finished something and somehow that experience broke the quitter off of my life.

When the Chancellor of the school laid hands and prophesied over me that day, he declared me a finisher. Since that time, I have finished what I have put my hands to do. I have since graduated with my Masters, and you are now reading my Doctoral thesis. Fathers prepare you to finish if you will pursue the relationship with all of your heart.

Accessing All Your Heart

Love the Lord your God with all your heart and with all your soul and with all your strength. -Deuteronomy 6:5

Many sons find that what they previously thought what was "all", amounted to only "some." There is more inside the son than the son could ever see because he operates on a limited perspective of self by God's design. The son, living in independence for 20 years, pursuing their best, forging through the wilderness will find 20 months with a God-assigned fathering leader to be more productive than the previous 20 years. This is why the enemy fights this so hard against fathering relationships. One cannot love God with all until he can access all. What part of the son's life is off limits is a constant fathering curiosity.

Though I discuss this further in Seasons of Invitation, the son was designed with a fathering leader in mind. The disciple needs a master; the son needs a father. During the pursuit of a fathering leader, greater heart chambers open, and sons will have to learn to love with more. Learning to love with more will further empower the pursuit. As the "more" expands, sons begin to learn a greater understanding of who and what they are and who they are after, the "voice within the voice."

Access Granted

I will place on his shoulder the key to the house of David; what he opens no one can shut, and what he shuts no one can open. Isaiah 22:22

A fathering leader will have access to give or withhold from a son. Like giving keys, the son should realize that access is granted and should never be presumed. Presumption that stems from pride will always test the boundary of a son's authority. A son isn't a door opener, but an obedient follower through doors that are opened. This empowers the son to be ready as a father to avoid self-promotion and for him to be one who allows God to open doors that no man can close when he stands as a father to other sons.

Self-promotion is rampant and is all over the mainstream church due to an ambition that is not only tolerated, but it is also often celebrated. Pastors that have tremendous ambition are often the first hired. If not corrected, their un-executed ambition will execute their divine promotion. They may get something, but it won't be inheritance. They may appear successful, but it is often as the world would define it, missing the purpose of God for them all together.

Fathers grant access because they are able to measure when the son is ready to walk through another door. It is always a safeguard for a son to be a door holder, rather than a door opener. On the other side of sonship, these fathers will understand what it is like to wait on the Lord for years behind a door that God has promised rather than open a door themselves or allow another to hold open a door that they can later close. These fathers have learned that God does not withhold good things to mature sons who have trusted in Him for timing.

The Impossible Pursuit

The pursuit of a fathering leader is impossible in the natural. That impossibility requires the son to learn to lean into Holy Spirit's power. That impossibility stays imprinted as a successful pursuit breeds a heavier reliance. When striving, the son will fail. The father will walk through the failure and mine out overlooked treasure that was hidden by pain. When running in soul rest, the son will succeed. Learning to allow the breath of the Spirit to blow the breeze of God into the lungs of the runner teaches the son to move and live, to be bent and not broken. This multiplies hunger and thirst and brings a filling when the son realizes there is nothing in this for him.

That does not bring defeat; it brings forth a great victory. The son realizes that as ambition has been outrun, Holy Spirit will empower him to enter the place of faithful obedience being measured by what matters. The son does not see his service to God as performance, rather as the great joy of his life's work. The son doesn't fall into the trap of measuring success as the world does, but runs to hear the words "well done."

The son realizes that the outcomes are a bi-product of the revelation of a new nature that is being worked out from within. This is the place where identity manifests in good works that prove the nature that is hidden. The things performed, those exploits that are mile markers in the seasons of sonship, are not at an attempt to earn something already granted, but are simply what happens when a son of God lives in the earth.

2 THE PILLAR OF POSTURE

Blessed are the meek, for they will inherit the earth. -Matthew 5:8

The next pillar of sonship that empowers sonship progression that leads to expanded stature is the pillar of posture. Where pursuit is the kingdom cultural principle of hunger expressed in the son, posture is the kingdom cultural principle of humility. In the same way as sons will come face to face with God in grand ways when they pursue Him and the fathering leader He has assigned, the pillar of posture will ensure right relationship when encountered and proper connection through each season. It will also ensure the necessary transfer occurs as correct attitude will ensure the anointing will flow.

The right posture in a son is a safeguard and provides tremendous opportunities in breakthrough when mastered. With all the pillars, intentionality is of the utmost importance. Since Fathering leadership is the heartbeat of discipleship, this pillar ensures a clear understanding throughout the process of proper roles. What is easy in concept is often far harder to walk out in practice. This is true of sonship posture.

The Approach

But by the grace of God I am what I am, and his grace to me was not without effect. No, I worked harder than all of them—yet not I, but the grace of God that was with me. -1 Corinthians 15:10

Paul defines humility as merely being who he is by God's grace; nothing more and nothing less. It takes into consideration that proper humility is a grace release enhancer. Grace here is not mercy; it is the supernatural ability to do something that cannot be done without it. This can be seen clearly in the life of Paul, and it is in those moments that Paul's fathering heart came through loudest in his letters.

Paul refused to be anything other than what God's grace dictated. Grace is always released at the target of true identity as part of God's original design. If Holy Spirit did not take Paul somewhere, Paul did not go, as the necessary grace would be lacking for the completion of his apostolic assignment. However, much of Paul's time with God, 17 years before he ever was separated into his apostolic *metron* in Acts 13, grace limitations were a distinct focus in the school of Holy Spirit. Posture was the first thing Paul ever learned as he was knocked down and blinded after encountering Jesus.

And so it was with me, brothers and sisters. When I came to you, I did not come with eloquence or human wisdom as I proclaimed to you the testimony about God.
1 Corinthians 2:1

If any man could have come with something else, it would have been Paul! Considering his training over the course of years when known as Saul, he had been in training his entire life. He talks about this when he says that he was born on the 8th day. Paul gives a rundown of how he met the criteria of a great leader by the world's standards and yet, he gave that up for grace. It doesn't mean that these things never came into play with Paul, but it does mean that he learned not to put his trust in them.

To go further, Paul is sent to the Greeks. His education becomes less important to those to whom he is assigned. This is evidence that Paul was willing to take all of his experience and training as a Pharisee of Pharisees, spiritual son to a strict and honored leader in his day before Christ and consider it as "rubbish" for the cause of Christ. What he realized was that grace is what was needed. Grace would do in and through Paul what all these other things failed to do.

Paul desired the foundation of those who received his powerful words to rest upon their faith in Christ, not in him. This is evidence of a healthy posture. This posture allows the son to be comfortable in not being central to his or her ministry and produces the ability to find fulfillment in simple obedience, which makes Jesus central. This kind of posture finds it acceptable to leave the results to God and further safeguards against the enemy's attempts at defining success in the life of a spiritual son.

> *I know what it is to be in need, and I know what it is to have plenty. I have learned the secret of being content in any and every situation, whether well fed or hungry, whether living in plenty or in want.*
> *-Philippians 4:12*

Again Paul is talking through grace mechanics - how grace works, what it does, how it arrives, and what is produced from it. Grace empowers Paul's life and ministry. Even the gifts of the spirit are translated "works of grace." Again, this is not mercy or hyper-grace. Grace does not grant permission to sin; it enables us to win! Paul is willing to allow the grace of God to work within Him and not to allow any remaining pride to poach his purpose and desires to impart this understanding into his spiritual children.

Shared Posture

This is true, as Timothy's posture in sonship is so easy to discern within the text. Paul makes a contrast to Timothy, and other spiritual sons by saying, that only Timothy sought the things of Christ while the "others," sought their own thing. Timothy would have learned this in close proximity to Paul, and then as he was separated to his fullest leadership role, it would have been part of how he related to his assignment leading the very church that Jesus' mother attended, as well as the apostles. That is pressure you need to be prepared for!

Timothy didn't think of himself higher than he ought. One of the things that made the greatest difference in Timothy's life was to safely and securely rest upon the pillar of posture. The greatest gifts flourish where a strong pillar of posture is present. Logically, if these gifts work by grace, then the releaser of such gifts realizes that they are the worker but not the giver. This is no different from a pizza delivery boy realizing they don't deserve compliments of how delicious the pizza is that they just delivered. Their role was **not to make it,** but to **deliver it**.

The pillar of posture ensures the delivery boy does not subtly fall victim to thinking they should be a chef and then starting up their own pizza chain. This is how pride works when the pillar of posture is weak; it always opposes the work of grace. Pride is always the son's biggest internal adversary.

> *Likewise you younger people, submit yourselves to your elders. Yes, all of you be submissive to one another, and be clothed with humility, for "God resists the proud,*
> *But gives grace to the humble." Therefore humble yourselves under the mighty hand of God, that He may exalt you in due time,*
> *-1 Peter 5:5-6*

Humility in practice, is the outworking of a healthy pillar of posture founded within a spiritual son. It assures him that God will not resist him due to pride. Within this, the idea is that with a strong pillar of posture the son will not need to be opposed because the son will understand that his lifting up will not be his focus.

The lie is that if it isn't the son's focus, it is nobody's focus. This a struggle within sonship, and why it produces the necessary environment for these things to surface. If the son believes no one desires for him to be lifted, somewhere there is an open the door to that lie that has become a work of Hell within him. It is scriptural that God desires to lift His son as the son humbles himself.

It is true with Jesus who now has a place higher than any other as He humbled Himself even to die upon a cross. This is one of the most significant struggles within sonship and indicates an orphan. The son feels that he should be in control of his elevation, and that is a prideful presumption. God pushes down and raises. Don't fall victim to the lie that a fathering leader will never cooperate with the promotion of a son!

Even if the fathering leader is unhealthy, the reality is that submission in sonship produces heaven's involvement like nothing else. All of heaven is shouting and celebrating the submitted son; to see the glory of God revealed within the raising! Upon the platform of promotion, the sound of the submitted son glorifies Jesus, as the fathering leader's involvement makes Jesus more involved in the process than ever before.

Be Intentional

While the son is intentional about the correct posture with a fathering leader, the father is in control of timing in positioning. There is no issue here as long as the pillar of posture stands firm as upon it the need to perform cannot stand.

This is the correct way for a son to approach a spiritual father. The son knows that by God's assignment, this leader that God has chosen is to be a spiritual father. As the son honors this assignment and submits to it; he is submitting to God. That submission produces powerful fruit in both father and son. The son intentionally postures himself to elevate his fathering leader to the proper place.

Symptoms Of Improper Elevation

It is an unrealistic expectation that Spiritual Fathering Leaders will replace and heal the wounds of natural fathers, and yet that is one of the greatest motivators for wounded sons to elevate their fathering leader improperly. However, the Spiritual Fathering leader will often work to steady the unsteady son long enough for the power of God to reach the open wounds left by the natural father.   There will always be a temptation for a spiritual son to view their spiritual fathering leader as a natural father replacement, and this can lead to some problems as it is outside the purpose of the relationship.

If your natural father abandoned you, your unhealed wounds will often work against your fathering leader when they do not live up to some unrealistic expectation is inconsistent with their role. Spiritual Fathering leaders don't always remember your birthday. If your father was abusive, you might tend to see your spiritual fathering leader with paranoia, waiting for them to "come down" on you for not performing. If your natural father wasn't a man of his word, you might struggle with trust. It goes on and on.

Spiritual fathering leaders do have tremendous "identificational impact" in the relationship at strategic times of ministry. Often, these leaders can declare over a son or daughter a Father's blessing that deeply touches the very fabric of identity. They "step into" a role where they can represent natural fathers, but they primarily function is representation of the Heavenly Father. Because of this representation, sons should avoid pitfalls in relating to these representatives.

Subtle Fathering Pitfalls

There are subtle fathering pitfalls that sons can bypass to speed up their sonship progression. There will be discussed below. Avoiding the pitfalls ensures that energy can be better spent, and less time taking trying to get out of something that has no value. Traps exist on the path but don't have a purpose.

Idolization – A spiritual fathering leader is never a replacement deity. It is a grave error for a son to turn a spiritual fathering leader into a graven image, a replica of some being that has the power to grant wishes and make all things work out according to their desire. A spiritual fathering leader is called and empowered by Holy Spirit to be a representative of Jesus' leadership who desires to be present, not replaced. This is what a spiritual fathering leader does at many different levels, represents so that the son has more access to the leadership of Jesus than ever before! Sometimes, in the process, God will be most active when the fathering leader is least available.

People have the unfortunate ability to make idols out of anything. Israel did. Christians do. When you read about Israel's witchcraft problem carefully, you can see it even extended to the brazen serpent. Called the *Nehushtan*, the rod that was used as part of a prophetic action to bring healing to the Israelites who came under God's judgment in the wilderness, became an idol of witchcraft worship!

Fathers are not the Pope. Sons will trust them, believe in them, honor them, confide in them, and in many ways, Fathers will receive supernatural grace to represent Jesus. They are not magical! You don't buy a Father or rent a Father. You don't sow money into a Father so that they can do something for you that you must do for yourself! You don't pay a fathering indulgence, so you can sin more, submit less, and complain at an international level! A fathering leader will say, "Sit down and shut up" while representing the God of Heaven who is doing the same thing.

Good fathers will help break idols in the lives of their sons, even if they are that idol. One of the most significant ways for fathers to pummel that idolatrous image is to ignore. Ignoring a son provides the pressure a son needs to understand how they are relating with a father and if there are unhealthy things at work in how the son understands the relational dynamics. Silence in sonship speaks volumes. Throughout the seasons, silence will place the necessary pressure on the son for the level of reliance on the Heavenly Father behind the spiritual father to be adequately represented.

Imitation – Though at some points a son can and should represent a Fathering leader, a son should not imitate that Fathering leader. A good father will never desire a son to emulate them regarding the flesh; that is: mannerisms, assignments, etc. Though it is quite natural to share spiritual DNA within the assignment, a son shouldn't act, talk like, and dress like a fathering leader. This can quickly empty the relationship of the power because it is connecting upon the wrong basis. Spiritual Fathering connection is just that, spiritual. If you are connecting in the spirit, what is shared that is spiritual will not be a work of the flesh, but a work of God.

This is subtler than many realize. Often due to inadequate identity understanding within a son, the son sometimes can believe that they have discovered themselves when they found a father, and this is not true. A spiritual fathering leader will not give a son an identity. A son already has identity written by God. A son will, however, be positioned like never before to receive the understanding of what that identity is within healthy fathering leadership. The fathering leader will begin the process through discipleship of chipping away at the false that is inconsistent with the original purpose and is why connecting with a spiritual fathering leader is the beginning of a process, not the end of one.

Intimidation - Although this is quite common, a spiritual son should not be intimidated by a spiritual Fathering leader. The desire of the Fathering leader should be that the son fulfills all that the son has been given to do. The son running his race does not diminish the father's race even though if the son's race exists within the father's or vice-versa. The Father desires the son to run and win. This can help clarify the call. Intimidation points to a fear of man issue.

The point of fathering leadership is the exact opposite and will work to instill the Fear of the Lord at the onset. There will be more discussion about the fear of man vs. the fear of the Lord in the Season of Invitation. If your leader desires you to be intimidated by them, seek the Lord for a new leader; who sees you as a creation of Jesus, that you may be all God is calling you to be.

These three pitfalls can be subtle and are often blind spots to sons. It takes a higher perspective to see them many times, so trust in the fathering relationship will produce opportunities for greater freedom, healing, deliverance, and identity. Without being dealt with, these pitfalls will work against the four areas of sonship surrender introduced in chapters five through eight which are: **Transparency**, the son's willingness to be uncovered. **Training,** the son's willingness to trust in a training pathway that at times may appear inconsistent with their understanding of personal purpose. **Testing,** the son's willingness to learn endurance and endure testing required for increased stature. **Timing,** the son's ability to rest in a fathering leader's timing.

Posture Paces in Sonship

We are hard-pressed on every side, yet not crushed; we are perplexed, but not in despair; persecuted, but not forsaken; struck down, but not destroyed— always carrying about in the body the dying of the Lord Jesus, that the life of Jesus also may be manifested in our body.
2 Corinthians 4:8-10

Let's conclude this chapter by discussing the posture paces, or how fathering leaders will work with sons specifically on strengthening this critical pillar. Sons must go through the posture paces. The fathering leader needs to be approached as the pace setting leader in your life.

As my fathering leader has said to me, "Son, I am going to walk with you through this, not run." This is just because your posture with your fathering leader has produced the kind of perspective where he/she can set the pace to be consistent with your purpose and understands by the oversight of your soul what you need to walk through to be ready.

Without clarity on the mission that God shrouds in mystery, you cannot understand the proper pace without a pace setting leader. Timothy had to be ready to walk through his own 2 Corinthians 4:8-10 because that kind of persecution was not unusual when a church was in conflict with the culture of that time. Timothy needed to be ready to lead as a fathering leader in the midst of it.

Pressed Down

Many times, in a fathering leadership relationship, you feel you should be celebrated, but instead, you will be concealed. Your fathering leader will press you down because many times you won't be ready for your next season unless you become okay with not being seen. If you're not okay with not being seen, you won't authentically represent when you are seen because the need to be seen and celebrated is not the behavior of a mature son and points to unhealed places. Remember: you're inheriting something, not earning an allowance.

The enemy will attempt to convince you that your leader is overlooking over you when your leader is actually overseeing you. By understanding that the opposite is true, by not agreeing with the unhealthy motivations that birth the need to be celebrated, used, etc., the leader is representing the same behavior as God is exhibiting, investing their agreement in the places within you consistent to who you are. There will be more on this concept in, The Season of Invitation.

Pushed Forward

When a son faces rampant insecurity, the temptation to step back presents itself. Your pillar of posture, however, allows your fathering leader the right to push you forward when everything within you is screaming to retreat. The fathering leader is aware, and not afraid of a son's insecurity on any level and, in fact, can see aspects of instability the son may have considered a part of their personality. This is one of the most powerful elements of the fathering leader!

I recall one particular moment when my wife and I had just gone through a tragedy on a Saturday evening. After several attempts at pregnancy, we experienced another painful miscarriage. My spiritual father heard the news and called me that day. He said to me, "Son, I know this is hard, but you are going to preach tomorrow, and you are not going to preach out of your hurting emotions, you are going to release something out of your spirit."

Many other leaders I know would have instructed me to take the day off, be home with my wife and heal. Likely, my wife, and I would have stayed home and just stayed home without any healing happening. Instead we got up by God's grace and went to minister together. We could have resisted that day and said no as we had that right, and he would have let me. Instead, we realized that our fathering leader saw something we could not see, and needed to trust his leadership even when it hurt the most.

The Lord used me mightily and something special happened, out of my spirit came the sound of a healing victory that my soul walked into as I released it. My wife and I now have two beautiful children, 10 and 4. When your leader Is pushing you forward, but as a son, you feel the need to step back, the mature son approaches the Lord with an open heart to determine why the leader is seeing something different than the son is feeling.

The immature son thinks it is because the fathering leader doesn't consider his feelings, but it is because the fathering leader sees something! To them, it is clear and robust. To the son, he must be sometimes pushed and into something that is a mystery to him because he cannot see the purpose behind it. The mature son learns to not resist, but to rest. The fathering leader appreciates through the seasons as the "push forward" becomes a "pull back" as passions ablaze.

Perplexed

Paul says he has learned to be perplexed but not to the point where there is no hope. In sonship, when times of being perplexed come, the opportunity for a real hope that exists only in the Lord will arrive. Why would a fathering leader protect his son from being puzzled when it is so useful in preparation? This is why a fathering leader will walk a son into situations as an onlooker where the son is shocked because his father still has hope! Why? How? It is because the fathering leader has been here before, and God has shown Himself consistently faithful. The son can lean into the fathering leader's track record of faithfulness.

The son begins to walk with his leader and sees God come through and faith within him arises. The fathering leader is vulnerable during this process to the imperfections of humanity, but the risk is worth the son learning to put their trust in a God who is faithful. In this way, the son learns to be in these situations where it would appear all hope is lost and yet realizes that with God all things are impossible.

The son has to learn that nothing that can be seen around him can become the source of his hope. This is why so many ministers are leaving the ministry today; they have no desire. They are heart-sick and leave the ministry full of sickness. Having never learned from a fathering leader the tyranny of man's expectations, they die at the hand of their congregations who work them to death with little reward.

Cast Down

Faithful fathers walk their sons through failure. The son whose father always hides them from facing the reality of their failures prepares their sons never to be fathers. Failure happens in the life of every leader big or small. What one learns to do with failure, learns from failure, and advances out of failure will make the difference between the mature and immature. Many spiritual sons have never learned from failure as it was either blatantly hidden, overlooked, or ignored. These sons are often one defeat away from quitting and wasting eternal purpose.

Father's don't fear failure in their sons. They should feed passion, ensuring messes occur. These messes provide the most significant teaching opportunities the sons can have. Fathers who have not taught their sons both to succeed and to fail have not prepared their sons to reach the fullness of their destiny. Upon leaving the place of sonship into their place of being fathers, these sons will crack and lead out of their souls upon their first failure and possibly spend the rest of their lives leading from the wound left behind. A son who always has to find a way to redefine a failure as a success is immature. A son can't be a father until the idea of failure no longer causes him to hesitate.

Posture & Pursuit Working Together

A healthy posture empowers an aggressive pursuit of the desires of God in the life of a son. The mass mentality abundant in culture is that "it doesn't take all that." This ungodly mindset won't hinder a son who has these pillars in place. Those who say that a son should make a name for himself are stating that God won't be true to His word and raise the son up at the right time. Son's pursue their leader with the understanding that they represent a God in their lives in a way that brings them into alignment so that the involvement of God in their lives reaches the highest.

Where others experience an occasional breakthrough, sons that have these pillars in place consistently break through barrier after barrier. They realize that the grace that empowers their pursuit is not their power, and is available because they have submitted themselves to the seasons of sonship. They breakthrough because they realize that their trust is not in their ability or talent, but because they are acknowledging, in real ways, the God who has brought them into this relationship will honor it as He does in all other places He arrives and is welcomed, bringing fullness.

Intentional Posture

The mature son is intentional about posture. Ensuring who is greater is a tactical maneuver. Oil always flows down. The son who prioritizes posture positions himself as a landing pad for the anointing. This has been a true marker of what God has shown me this last decade.

As I have seen many others go pursue the anointing at various times and in various conferences, my posture has positioned me, so that God could get His desires delivered to me through my leader in the place I belong. I began to intentionally exercise this discipline and started monitoring results and have grown to the place where now not only my spiritual father, but anyone he sends to represent, can release whatever God desires. I have even had others tell me that the way I postured myself, making them "greater," in the moment, has had them function in an entirely new level.

They have been shocked with how powerfully the anointing moves through them because I am willing to let others be greater than me. I have learned to posture myself in a way where God can position those I lead to be more significant than me at certain times and release powerfully as a way to draw out the anointing. They say, that it is always easier to pray for me. I watched this dynamic about intentional honor redefine many around me. I also believe this is one of the ways we can measure a great maturity disparity within the body of Christ.

Today, in most places, if a well-known speaker comes into a ministry, the amount of hunger and honor skyrocket which is not something to be proud of, but to mourn over. If Kingdom Culture is mature within a ministry, there will be enough honor among the leaders in the house, that God can do whatever He desires. He doesn't need to send in a "professional" to get something done if we disciple kingdom citizens in the pillar of posture. Sons know how to honor what God sends, so they can receive everything He has, at any moment He desires.

3 THE PILLAR OF PERSPECTIVE

Every aspect of sonship must operate from a place of grace empowerment. For this to be true, the entire relationship between a fathering leader and a son has to be established by the will of God, not the will of man. When this is true, Holy Spirit operates in both individuals, investing Heaven's best to see the will of God happen. This works best when the pillar of perspective is clearly understood. Without the pillar of perspective operating within the son, the level at which the father can see, and the level of which the son can understand, diminishes.

Heavenly Father never forces fathering relationships, but they are always His desire because discipling is His strategy for transformation. All transformation is restoration. God doesn't force fathering just as He doesn't force anything else that occurs within the "realm" of free will. There are millions of God's children wandering around the world carrying some level of the Orphan spirit in areas of their heart that they alone have been unable to access. As long as there is Orphan within them, they cannot inherit. God desires them to walk with a fathering leader to write upon their hearts, prepare them and position them, for their inheritance.

These children are unable to see what is necessary by God's loving design. The way that creation has unfolded through Jesus's brilliant act brings together an understanding of a required interconnectivity built-in to His plan. At all times, among all people, someone can see more from the outside than from the inside, and a higher perspective will provide a different view. The fact that God, with the highest and deepest perspective of all, is willing to share His perspective should overwhelm His people with sincere gratitude.

Come Up Here

After these things I looked, and behold, a door standing open in heaven. And the first voice which I heard was like a trumpet speaking with me, saying, "Come up here, and I will show you things which must take place after this." -
Revelation 4:1

When John the Apostle is called up from the island of Patmos to see, hear, understand and communicate the book of revelation, He is pulled into a perspective far above his own. From this perspective, John can experience what had before been off limits to that degree. The way John interacts with the revelation tells us that even for him, it was likely a new experience or at least a "higher" level. Even as the beloved of the lamb of God often with his head upon Jesus' chest, it appears He had not had such an experience before.

"By the Spirit" is the way a Fathering leader can prioritize a son's purpose while seeing from a higher perspective, enabling the son to prioritize the posture and pursuit. The fathering leader does not get a higher perspective because of his rigorous training, study, prayer life, passion, etc. Those things prepare the father so that he can understand what is being seen. The perspective over the life of a son or daughter is one that is granted, not one that is gained by other religious measures, no matter how honorably they are stewarded.

The fathering leader sees from the perspective God grants over the life of a son; while the son can impact the level at which the fathering leader can see! This concept makes sense when the substantial requirement of grace is upon all aspects of the relationship. Perspective, just like posture, pursuit, and purpose, works by grace that is released from the Holy Spirit. The son must agree for the father to see!

The Oil Of Honor

By far one of the least understood concepts in today's church is that of honor. On one side of the coin, you have those who understand honor as control and domination, and couldn't be further from the true definition of honor in the Kingdom. Flip the coin, and you have a different problem, no honor at all, which typically comes from being hurt from the other side of the coin. Honor is far too important to neglect. You cannot have Kingdom without honor in proper operation.

But in a great house there are not only vessels of gold and silver, but also of wood and clay, some for honor and some for dishonor. -2 Timothy 2:20

Honoring a fathering leader is merely agreeing with God about who He says they are as a spiritual father and what they carry as a treasury. The level of honor exhibited in the son's posture will empower their perspective.

He who receives a prophet in the name of a prophet shall receive a prophet's reward. And he who receives a righteous man in the name of a righteous man shall receive a righteous man's reward. -Matthew 10:41

If a son only honors a fathering leader as a great person, he can receive from a father's experience and expertise. This type of relationship can be understood as mentoring or coaching. If a son honors his leader as sent from God, it increases their perspective by receiving them as a representative of Jesus. This perspective is not "worship," as the fathering leader does not get "all honor" as Jesus does, but gets "appropriate honor" as one sent to represent.

The spiritual dynamic at play results in the fathering leader being a storehouse or treasury of what God desires to deposit into the life of a son through it.

Appraisal

Sons must have a proper fathering valuation; not an evaluation. Sons don't select; they submit to God's selection, which comes from a biblical understanding of honor defined as "ascribing or attributing value or an appraisal." That means a son sets the value of what is in their life but should set the value separately based upon what they secure and what God sends. Consider the purchase of a home as an example of this concept. If a person is willing to pay a "fair" price for a home, it is what the value of the home is to them. That doesn't always equal market value, sometimes it far exceeds it.

The market value of fathers in the Kingdom is high and all Kingdom leaders should be valued according to what God says about them! Imagine if someone were to purchase a home to live in that was somewhat of a good fit for their lifestyle. If this were the case, they would pay market value and no more. If there were a higher demand for that home, people would pay much more than the market average because of how they perceived the value, demand, and opportunity. Now, imagine that home sat on top of a large pile of gold that became known to one of the buyers. They might double or triple the purchase price because of what was underneath it.

This is a simple picture of how honor works in fathering. What a son values is not the leader, alone, but also what fills them and who sent them. While all leaders receive some honor, the leader God assigns as a Fathering leader should receive more! As long as sons honor in conjunction to who, and what, God is carrying in that leader for their life, the leader will remain full with a divinely empowered perspective. This gives that leader tremendous vision for their son consistent with purpose. If the value falls, what is in the "house" lessens.

"…and be renewed in the spirit of your mind," -Ephesians 4:23

When Paul the Apostle prays that the Ephesian church is renewed in the spirit of their mind, he asks for something staggering to occur. The word "renew" in this passage is where we get the word "renovate." Paul desires that the Holy Spirit will renovate their mind's interior so that the people can understand proper value. They will know the perfect will of God by doing it! In other words, they will value what God values and do what God does. Holy Spirit renovates the mind to value, and that is what He does in the relationship with a fathering leader.

When Paul also prays that the "eyes of their heart be enlightened," in Ephesians 1, he uses a powerful Greek word. The word is where we get the English word, *"photo",* and it paints a picture of a bright light that brings clarity to the surroundings. This is the light of encounter, how they could know how God feels about them. A great example of this a particular species of fish that lives at such depths that there is no need to have physical eyes. Paul is declaring at that level, that this burst of illuminating light would break into the experience of these believers, and that they would experience the encounter that produces the knowledge that comes from experiencing something.

Holy Spirit is renewing the mind to sonship so that sons can know the heart of the father in the deep dark places lurking within their own hearts. When this happens, rooms that seemed small open up as doors become visible to entirely new surroundings. Sons can feel free to wander and explore. This is the light that God is releasing into sons today. There are doors previously undiscovered with treasure on the other side.

The Key of Honor

The Son has the key to lock or unlock the vast spiritual treasury within a fathering leader by determining the level of honor to carry! No matter how much the fathering leader desires to release the plans of God into the son as revealed in each season, the fathering leader does not alone, hold the key.

At each stage, to the level the father can see, the son can be. The perspective or " blueprint," can be stored within the fathering leader who has been "fitted," but honor unlocks the revealing of it in the son who is being "shaped." As proper honor empowers a divine perspective, consistent and supernatural revelation can arrive into the son from the fathering leader.

It does not eliminate the revelation the son receives from the Lord; instead, it increases the revelation as the son matures throughout the seasons of sonship. As things progress, the son will become a significant source of revelation as the process, itself, increases stature that correctly honors revelation. Many sons struggle with honor, but honor is a weapon in the hands of a mature son. By wielding it well, sons can receive from God in the place they have been positioned, without the need to go looking for it elsewhere.

Immediately, this begs the question of why so many sons disconnect from leadership. The reason, on a rather large scale, is that they did not master the pillar of perspective, honoring their leader to the extent their leader's effectiveness could assist them in moving through the needed healing that ends up making them run. They despise God's provision and then unintentionally lock-up their fathering treasury. They stop receiving and then wonder why they seem to be plagued with ineffectiveness.

The pursuit outside of the fathering relationship that God assigned leads them towards distraction which will pull them to invest in substitutes. Substitutes lead to separation; separation leads to waste. The purpose that was meant to be never materializes, the baby never born. The idea that It will just happen has pushed many disconnected children to dead ends in a land of waste.

Pursuing The Perspective

The son's proper pursuit is after the perspective of the fathering leader, not just a relationship with the fathering leader. Powerful! The fathering leader, by design, can see further and more comprehensively. The son, honoring this within a fathering leader, empowers a perspective that consistently leads to astonishing breakthroughs. Awareness of this fact will help keep things from becoming familiar. Familiarity is the enemy of honor. It becomes a massive threat with more time, which means each of these pillars must be solidly in place within each season.

When a car buyer finds a car he desires he can go to great lengths to purchase it. At first, considerable effort goes into maintaining it, cleaning it, and driving it. Over time, the car is revalued as merely a way to get from one place to another. As more time passes, it becomes a car payment and then a burden. The wear and tear of the vehicle becomes more evident but doesn't bother the owner. Why? The answer is familiarity. The car has become common because a lack of intentionality.

Washing a new car is enjoyable, as pride in ownership makes dull tasks celebrated. Over time, the upkeep can become monotonous. Unless the car owner consistently and intentionally remains grateful, the car will never remain as a treasure in the eye of the owner, which can be true in fathering leadership is the reason why perspective is so important. Familiarity seeks to rob the treasury within the fathering leader; mature sons won't allow it.

Double Honor

Sons that don't maintain the proper honor for fathering leaders forget they are honoring who sent them and what is in them. Un-Intentionality can be deadly in the relationship. If the son starts relating on any other merit than the one the father represents, such as giftedness, experience, or call, they can soon lose the perspective that allows for double-honor.

Let the elders who rule well be counted worthy of double honor, especially those who labor in the word and doctrine.
-1 Timothy 5:17

One level of honor is the person, and that honor exists among believers everywhere. God loves His creation, and so all should honor that. Another level of honor above that empowers the perspective described. If the honor held becomes about anything else, it is far too easy to lose. If a son honors a fathering leader because he never seems to fail, a big enough failure will test the pillar of perspective. If the pillar doesn't hold true, all that has been built upon it will inevitably fall.

Improper honor for a leader based upon his preaching ability, ministry growth capability, vision sharing, marriage, family, etc., can strike and shake the pillar. If any of the pillars shake hard enough, what God is building in the relationship will begin to collapse. If the son expects the fathering leader to start explaining himself, the battle is already lost. Honor is far more valuable than appreciation but both have a place.

Embracing The Mystery

Mature sons must learn the art of embracing mystery. God is mysterious, and if thinking God must always explain Himself becomes engrained in the son, the fruit of this truth will not be held. At some point in the future, the son will be tested and shaken when God refuses to explain Himself. God says, "Go" and the sons says, "No." The "No" will not necessarily sound like that, but it will be a "No," none the less. At this stage, it sounds like an expectation for God to explain Himself that results in hesitancy.

The son, here, feels entitled, and that comes because of pride. Pride in all forms hinders sonship because God resist it. When God opposes a son, the fathering leader will cooperate with that resistance, even at great pain to himself. The fathering leader watches as the son wrestles and tries to hold the son steady as long as the Lord will allow. The discipline does not come directly from the fathering leader, but their involvement is to encourage the son to endure.

Many Prophets have fallen into the mystery trap. Prophets by God's design and mandate love secrets but subtly can begin to believe they can know what God knows in every case. This is an excellent place for a plug for a prophetic company which teaches Prophets to work together in meekness, dealing with competition, envy, jealousy, insecurity, and the need to be celebrated. New Testament prophecy is a team sport.

Prophets who do not learn to become acquainted and even welcome mystery will tend to push into the hype, exaggeration, and worse, witchcraft to learn secrets. God has no interest in revealing redefining the function of a Prophet into a whisperer which divides chief friends. Having been part of three separate prophetic companies with my sonship process, I highly recommend all Prophets take part in them no matter their level of function.

Proper Expectation

Understanding proper expectation within a fathering relationship is essential. As previously mentioned, unrealistic expectations born out of past wounds can hamper the efforts of the Lord within the connection. Spiritual fathers are not natural fathers. If previous injuries create the hope that spiritual fathers will be around every birthday, holiday, etc. that requires celebration, the relationship will not function correctly.

Either the fathering leader who is immature will try to meet such demands, or they will by grace work to bring to the surface the reality of these unrealistic expectations in hope that the son can be corrected. A key to remember in sonship is this: always choose impact over interaction. High impact does not always equal lots of interaction, just as a loud volume doesn't necessarily mean many words.

The posture of the son here is imperative. Rather than the son putting expectations upon the father; the son should allow the father to train them about what expectations are realistic in the relationship. This will work in favor of a long-term relationship. Though the son is accountable, and the pursuit means working at being responsible, it does not mean that every communication will receive a timely response or a response at all.

Many times in my sonship, unanswered questions to my fathering leader have been answered by the Lord so that when my fathering leader finally responded to them, it was a confirmation to what I had already heard. If I was wrong, dialogue could show me why that was true in staggering ways. Remember that God is more involved in personal devotion when a fathering relationship is in place because it is His strategy. This means He honors the plan, and there is a synergy more magnificent than the individual parts. The proper expectations in sonship always tie to the purpose of the relationship existing in the first place.

The Heart Of A Father

I expect my fathering leader to have God's heart for me and to prioritize it over *his heart* for me. If God desires me to go through, my Fathering leader should be mature enough to prioritize his Father's heart for me above his own, and he should challenge me to move forward even if he wishes he could permit me to stop. This will be how I discover, as a son, that I am a conqueror and then even more than a conqueror! How can I learn that if my fathering leader falls to his own emotion and permits me to quit before the process is finished?

The reality of becoming victim to my own heart is challenged on many occasions, even in the fathering relationships I have with sons. I wish I could take them from the pressure and rescue them. I realize, however, that I am not the hero in this relationship, God is. I know that I am not the one as a father to get glory in what my sons become and do; Go is. I die to my desire and let Christ live in me with sons and daughters, even when I am sending them to "die their own deaths." I die in my fathering so Jesus can lead; they die within their sonship so Jesus can live.

The Mouth Of The Father

I expect my father to speak as an oracle of God and for Holy Spirit to fill my fathering leaders' mouth with words for me when I need them, even if I do not realize the need. These words arrive-sometimes soothing, sometimes striking, and always timely. I cannot expect them if I am not honoring the vessel, as God will fill what we agree upon. From the overflow of the heart, the mouth speaks. This doesn't mean we do not discuss routine matters, but I always keep my ears open to hear the voice within the voice.

As soon as Jesus was baptized, he went up out of the water. At that moment heaven was opened, and he saw the Spirit of God descending like a dove and alighting on him. And a voice from heaven said, "This is my Son, whom I love; with him I am well pleased." -Matthew 3:16-17

I listen with a heart-posture of honor, to hear, and feel God speak through regular communication with my fathering leader. Often, Holy Spirit will begin to minister to me from a conversation that happens via electronic means. He will come and breathe upon a standard text message, and that standard message becomes the booming voice of God as I have learned to tune into the "voice within the voice."

Because I have mastered this, my fathering leader can be halfway around the world, and there is no limitation. If I have the right perspective, he can speak to me because I have the proper posture, and the words to arrive with the power released in grace for me to accomplish what I need to do! This works even if what I need to do is to repent; there will be a grace for correction. There is no distance in the spirit, and because God is in the relationship, I trust the pulse of my heart is available to my father.

How I Am Intentional About Maintaining Honor

As I finish this chapter, I want to write about three strategic ways that I am intentional about honor. These personal protocols fight familiarity and ensure I have someone who can be a filled treasury of fathering in my life. While some say this is over-the-top, I am intensely intentional about what I value. Just as I have personal protocols that protect other relationships such as with my wife and family, I have those that defend my relationship with a spiritual father.

The Use Of Title

I never refer to my fathering leader by his first name. Never. I speak to him in honor. I call him "Dr. Don." He has never asked me to do this and others don't, but I do it on purpose. The reason I do is the same as why I utilize titles with those in 5-fold offices in the body of Christ. I use Apostle, Prophet, etc. to denote the fact that I realize and recognize that even though I could know them by their names (natural), I refuse to only understand them by that and seek to connect with what is within them.

Others do not do this, I do. When I call someone Apostle, I am making an honor demand. I am saying that the person is sent in the body of Christ, and that at any moment, God can put something in them for me that goes beyond how I know them naturally. I use this to agree with what God says about them. I do not want dishonor to limit what God desires to do in my life. At the same time, I refuse lip service, to receive it or release it. I will only speak consistently with what I see with the eyes of my heart. Any words outside of that are empty.

I also utilize "sir." This is not required, but even as I father others, they hear "sir" come out of me when referring to my fathering leader. By doing this, I am purposefully setting him in a place of honor in my heart. Sometimes, after a disagreement, these smalls things can help "reseat" a fathering leader in the son's heart.

Listen, Not Speak

When I am with my fathering leader, I never determine the tempo or course of the conversation until he gives me that license. I am always listening for "that sound" so by listening intently, I increase my chances of hearing that thing God can release at any time. With others, I do not do this. To those I lead, I lead in conversation. When I am led, the opposite is true. I ensure that the role of the relationship is clear. He is the father who has much to teach, I am the son with much to learn.

Again, this has never been an issue or demanded. At times, my fathering leader has needed me to speak more than I have, in those moments to hold back is to dishonor. I allow him to set the tempo and the course. If he sets a particular path, I am faithful to walk it. By doing this, I learn to prioritize the Lord's voice above all. God speaks in a whisper, so sons learn to hone their hearing so they can carry a thunder. By doing this, they can contain a voice more significant than their own.

Serve

I serve my fathering leader when the opportunity presents itself. Though I have honor with leaders personally, and am a father to them, I will intentionally serve my leaders in public. I will be the one to get the glass of water even if I am the speaker at the conference as well. Even if those in attendance do not understand the relational dynamic between us and incorrectly see us as equals, I will work on purpose to make him greater.

This protects my fathering leader by ensuring that he remains greater in my eyes. I will carry his bag if he will let me, but he doesn't really like that. I will open doors, ensure he has assistance to his vehicle, and build a strategy to honor him whenever I am able. I take his calls and very rarely ignore or avoid. Even if I do not feel like talking, I will answer the call as a way of honor as long as it doesn't violate other relational dynamics like with my family. If I must decline something that is offered, I do so in honor allowing him to understand how by being asked is an honor.

There are other ways in which I am very intentional about honor that will be discussed in the different seasons of sonship. Each season has protocol, process, and promise. Take an opportunity to ask Holy Spirit in the relationship with your spiritual father what small things you can do to fight the familiarity that comes over time. You also need strategic ways to ensure that in your heart, this vessel of honor never becomes a vessel for everyday use.

4 THE PILLAR OF PURPOSE

No one serving as a soldier gets entangled in civilian affairs, but rather tries to please his commanding officer.
-2 Timothy 2:4

The next pillar within sonship is the pillar of purpose. Within Kingdom culture, we would call this holiness. Holiness as in "set apart" can be understood in the corresponding question; set apart to what? The "what" can be understood in purpose. Within this context, the purpose is what a son was created to do that comes out of who the son was designed to be. This is the aim of fathering: for the son to be the vessel God created him to be so that He could pour out the purpose within him.

Within the context of Kingdom culture, holiness is paramount. The King is Holy, and there is none like Him. Sons do not dabble in the affairs of the world because they are holy like their King. The King has a purpose, and, therefore, every Kingdom citizen has a purpose within the larger one. The purpose can be discovered within the fathering relationship because it is one of the aspects of inheritance.

Understand inheritance as the man's purpose and the corresponding provision for that purpose to be realized. This would mean, however, that purpose cannot be received until the son is ready to inherit. This begs the question; how can a son pursue a purpose that has not yet been released to him? The answer is simple and yet sophisticated. The pursuit of faithfulness to a fathering leader matures the son and makes that son ready to inherit.

The purpose is part of the inheritance. The fathering leader, therefore, makes the son ready, developing through discipleship what God releases. The pursuit of the son is not towards an unrealized purpose or potential but towards the preparation of the purpose that can be seen through the eyes of the assigned fathering leader. This is a place where mystery enters into the relational dynamic and is secured by the other pillars of posture and perspective. The purpose is first seen through the eyes of a fathering leader while the son only receives glimpses of the goal during the pursuit. The glimpses become more grandiose as the goal gets closer!

Sons of the estate

As long as the son's purpose remains veiled in mystery, the son should pursue his father's purpose. Some have understood this as "serving another man's vision until receiving a personal vision," but this falls within the realms of Christianity's urban legend. No man has ever been given a ministry because they served a ministry. God doesn't work that way. Ministries are not obtained in that manner. The ministry of Jesus is not multi-level marketing.

The son's purpose exists within the father's purpose. This is how inheritance works. Using the natural world for example, in an agricultural setting, the son works the field that will one day be his. It is his while he is working it, but it will be his in a more significant way when he has the most authority and responsibility for it. The working of the ground doesn't earn the son the field as it will come to him as an heir. I will explain "imprints" in <u>Book Two, Season of Invitation</u> which brings clarity to what the son discovers within the father.

Working the field, however, does prepare for the son to learn what is required in the up-keep. While the father and the son are working in the field together, there is an excellent opportunity for expansion of the estate. One day, when the father can no longer labor, the son will be the father of sons who are learning the same skills to expand the estate even further. The son learns that aspects of the estate expansion increase on his watch, and this will continue forward with his sons.

God as a good father releases inheritance to Jesus who releases it to mature sons who expand it. These sons have developed through discipleship which at the heart level is to be understood as fathering. Sons must grow to reach the ultimate of purpose by prioritization of that purpose above all else. Discipleship at this level deals a deathblow to distraction which contrasts significantly with humanistic potential-pursuit.

The "any person can be anything and do anything at any time" idea is not from God. From God's book written before a son was created, with every particular included, a son does not have the freedom to define himself and do whatever feels is the best. The mature son prepares and prioritizes the purpose to the point of maturing to heirship. Once the son is an heir legally, in that he is not disqualified due to immaturity, he can inherit.

Immediately, this presents a challenge to be further discussed in the chapter on training. If a son of God has been trained based on potential, training based upon purpose can present quite the shock. Many sons have failed their training because they decided they would prefer to invest in potential rather than purpose. Investing in potential without a fathering perspective on purpose will ultimately lead to waste.

Formed and Forged

For you created my inmost being; you knit me together in my mother's womb.
-Psalm 139:13

Pastor Lisa Howard from Jacksonville, Florida, says "God saw that something needed to happen, and creating a son or daughter was how He would get it done." Every person ever created was created on purpose. The purpose put within each creation is the highest calling and justifies the creation's existence. The idea of "randomness" must be removed from the minds of sons and daughters.

Many who approach Jesus that call him Lord look so significantly different than their purpose that they are rejected when it counts the most. This is not absolute determinism, as if free will was not involved or people do not miss it. Of course, people miss it every day. If every person arose and accomplished their sole purpose, the earth would be vastly different.

The King of Glory would be represented thoroughly within culture across the nations as individual purposes harmoniously synchronized with others to create a massive orchestration that made Jesus' testimony broadcast throughout the heavenly places.

Then you will know the truth, and the truth will set you free." -John 8:32

How can a person reach purpose? The answer must begin with an understanding of discipleship. Discipleship is the strategy of God for fallen people, nations and creation to be transformed and therefore restored to what God originated by making God's power available.

The truth makes us free. This, of course, begins at the Cross, which cemented God's great victory and started man's journey towards realizing it personally. The cross of Jesus Christ, no matter how powerful, is not the end but the beginning. It was the end of His earthly race, but begins, and sustains ours. Purpose can be often overlooked as it resides deep within vessels that have given themselves over to dishonor or misuse.

Those vessels cannot see their purpose, although potential is clear. It is easier for those vessels to chart their trajectory based upon identified talent and gifting. Gifting does not always, however, point to purpose. It can very much lead away from it and is why sons should not chart their course to reach the objective.

Set Apart For A Purpose

Directly opposed to most moderns, the revelation of purpose does not first arrive in the mind of the person that holds that purpose. Shocking to some! Within the New Testament, there is not one character who owned the fullness of their purpose without someone else being aware of it first. Take, for example, Jesus' disciples. All of them had believed their occupation was purpose when it was potential's natural and cultural choice.

After not being selected for advanced learning under the rabbinical system of discipleship, the disciples were all involved in family professions as was common in those days. When Jesus arrived to call them, they were invested. They had no idea the height of their purpose. Even as they started to get grasps of it, Jesus saw the purpose as Father revealed to Him more clearly, which was the perspective He fathered from.

Jesus gave them this answer: "Very truly I tell you, the Son can do nothing by himself; he can do only what he sees his Father doing, because whatever the Father does the Son also does. -John 5:19

Jesus' understanding of His disciples' purpose came as a revelation from Father. This is how He functioned on the earth; a man filled with and controlled by the Holy Spirit. Jesus didn't know the specifics of these men because He was their creator. His fathering leadership to His disciples worked from the revelation of purpose empowered by Holy Spirit, as were all areas of His earthly ministry. He did this so we can do it!

While they were worshiping the Lord and fasting, the Holy Spirit said, "Set apart for me Barnabas and Saul for the work to which I have called them." -Acts 13:2

On The Other Side Of Pentecost

Paul is a strong example. Think through Paul's commissioning with Barnabas. Holy Spirit came to Paul's leaders first, which is kingdom normal. He instructed the leaders to separate Paul to purpose. How much a glimpse of this purpose Paul had before they separated him to it, we are not aware. However, we do know that Paul never separated himself, and he didn't prepare himself as if he had the details to purpose.

To take a silly natural example, imagine a 12-month-old baby standing in front of a mirror with an iPhone, taking a video to upload to YouTube, thoroughly discussing her purpose. The video would immediately become viral! For starters, the fact that the baby could hold the iPhone and figure out how to record would be striking. Secondly, the idea that any baby could understand that thoroughly, their purpose, would be hilarious to onlookers alike.

Many in the body feel they have a grasp of purpose and that God owes them a thorough explanation so they can manage the entire purpose pursuit. When the entire purpose doesn't come across clearly, they throw tantrums to try and leverage God into giving them the information they seek. When God doesn't answer them, they make it up as they go. Never even close to arriving before God as an heir because of their immaturity, they invest themselves in fantasy. In the <u>Season of Invitation,</u> infants learn to grasp, in <u>Interdependence</u>, they learn to interact.

Kept In the Dark

God was willing to keep Paul and Barnabas in the dark in the matters of purpose, and He does the same today. His strategy is to release this through leadership throughout scripture, and it stands to reason that today is no different. Just as children's parents understand, in varying ways, a child's purpose so that they can train the child in their particular way; spiritual fathering leaders operating by grace empowered gifting and spiritual perspective receive a greater understanding of purpose first.

The reason is simple. It makes submission a "must" to all parties. Fathering leaders submit to God to prioritize His will above their desire, while sons and daughters submit themselves to leaders so that they can arrive at purpose and take no credit. This submission gets grace moving their direction, and when grace arrives it doesn't just empower an understanding of purpose by the spirit, it empowers the pathway to purpose as the son and daughter walk the narrow way avoiding potential pitfalls.

Potential is the broad way, meaning that it does not require grace, and that striving will suffice. The purpose is the narrow way that isn't walked via effort alone, and where supernatural power is required. To navigate the pathway of purpose is impossible without divine empowerment. This is true by design. A fathering leader will receive God's passion for walking the right path . The same leader will oppose any effort that leads to waste.

A Glimmer Of Hope, Glimpses Of Purpose

As the son walks with a fathering leader and matures, the son receives more glimpses about his or her purpose. Often, these simple glimpses arrive in remarkable ways. There is nothing like maturing a son to see the truth of what power can be released within purpose. This will mark the maturing son and should empower a higher pursuit of purpose. This comes throughout the seasons of sonship and can tempt the son or daughter to run after these grand glimpses.

I have had some grand glimpses of personal purpose over the last ten years of sonship with my spiritual father. At first, they arrived only now and again, but they still landed powerfully shaking my spirit. As I have progressed in sonship stature, they arrive more consistently, more powerfully, and stay longer. I recall with great joy when I was sent out to prophesy in the nation of Brazil. I was being raised as a Prophet with this international leader and was finally submitting after a solid year of resisting the mantling of Prophet.

The conference there was over-the-top powerful as people experienced God's glory released in His word coming out of my mouth. As I watched them crumble under the weight of His word through me, I realized I could do that forever. "No more need to progress; I am here," I thought to myself. The word of God would land within me, bubble up, and then come forth like roaring waters. I felt so blessed to be used in that way.

However, my fathering leader continued to walk me into more uncharted territory over the next eight years. Every time I thought I reached the end and was solidly in the fullness of purpose more progression was required. Had it been up to me, I would have paused, stayed right there, and been happy. However, my fathering leader called me to emerge and pushed me to develop not only in the Prophetic, but then also the Apostolic. My function and life received greater grace to be who I was called to be.

Today, I am in securely planted in corporate purpose, and my hunger for completely managing my purpose has all but disappeared because I am at rest where I am. If the need arises for more progression, I am happy to receive the grace and cooperate with Holy Spirit through my leaders. If I stay here, I will be content in that as well. As I have progressed, I have learned that even though I am coming into agreement with this pillar of purpose, I am always at work cooperating with the Holy Spirit and leaders who help purify my purpose.

The Purification Of Purpose

Do nothing out of selfish ambition or vain conceit. Rather, in humility value others above yourselves, not looking to your own interests but each of you to the interests of the others. In your relationships with one another, have the same mindset as Christ Jesus: Who, being in very nature[God, did not consider equality with God something to be used to his own advantage; rather, he made himself nothing by taking the very nature of a servant, being made in human likeness. -Philippians 2 :3-7

Personal purpose is always purified when submitted to a higher purpose. Corporate purposes are more significant than personal, and national are higher than regional. Each time purpose is submitted to the level above it, it is purified. Again, back to the prophetic example, when an international Prophet works within a company and presents herself to a corporate function her purpose is refined. The Prophet should not only do this but also do it in a company that he/she does not lead.

Selfish ambition cannot live in this type of submitted lifestyle. Whatever aspects of personal purpose have selfish ambition within them need another level of fire and forge. Sons with selfish ambition or who suffer from vain conceit will not be ready to inherit as meekness marks the heir. The process of fathering exists to prepare the son to be a father, so God will deal forcefully with this reality in a son with impure personal purpose limiters.

This is why fathering leaders have such a supernatural discernment and perspective over a son's life and completely ignore potential. Potential is ignored because it will never produce purpose. It is a substitute, an enemy of God's purpose in life and will make up the total of the greatest sacrifice to purpose. Fathering teaches sons to sacrifice for purpose and potential is often the greatest of these sacrifices.

In the place of purpose

I had an experience in my own life where I was out of town at a conference for work and found out that there was a revival that was supposedly happening up in the northern part of the United States within driving distance of my hotel. I decided to rent a car and drive up and see if this was a true revival since I was already going to miss a strategic event in my home base with an international Apostle and Prophet. Within 20 minutes of arriving at this revival destination, though I discerned a lot of good things happening, I did not sense true revival.

Our Sunday services were honestly closer to revival than what I was experiencing. Since I felt discouraged with my investment (I am opposed to any waste in my life), I called the airline to see if there was any way the airline could get me home in time to be a part of the conference. The cost was steep, both monetarily and 4 hours of driving to another airport. I decided to prioritize the place of my purpose.

When I arrived the next day, having not slept, I ran into the conference as the speakers were saying their last goodbyes and praying one more time for the men in the ministry. I walked up front, and as the leaders quickly touched each man, they paused when they got to me. The Apostle asked me my name, and then began to prophesy to me. She said that though I did not understand why the fire was so hot in my life at that time, and though I had asked repeatedly to come out of the fire, it is because the weapon of purpose was being forged.

She then prophesied explicitly what the next three years of my life would be. I have often taken that prophetic word out to war with as a weapon. The truth of purpose is this: all the provision that needs to arrive for the purpose will arrive in the place of that purpose. The word I needed was not at some revival that had much attention; it came through me being in my proper place.

The Lifestyle Of Purpose

Upon the pillar of purpose, the lifestyle of the mature son, is made. This means, that things inconsistent with that purpose, are freely and willingly forfeited. While this becomes more specified in the later seasons of sonship, it is understood early on as the values of the fathering leader's assignment, and how that assignment is shared. Through trust, the fathering leader in a son's life can help guide to more significant areas of purpose. As that purpose is experienced being fulfilled, the son can experience the "well done" of sonship.

God is calling us to let go of our incomplete understanding of purpose. At times, this will feel as if God is asking us to sacrifice our Isaac. Even if it is true, God would still be worthy of such sacrifice. In this season, however, God often asks us to let go of an Ishmael we wish to rename Isaac and say, "Oh, that Ishmael could stand before you!" If we can't let go of purpose here, we won't be ready to surrender more when God asks. We as sons can hold the baby, but our fathers are willing to teach us how to pay the unthinkable cost of purpose.

Moving Towards Strategic Areas of Sonship Submission

The next chapters will cover four areas of sonship submission. These areas will prove to be vital in sons who want to progress more rapidly and connect with fathers who carry significant levels of Kingdom authority. These chapters will help the son choose tremendous impact over interaction and learn to love accountability, correction, and all aspects of the burden pursuit. With the pillars of sonship being firmly established, the four areas of sonship submission mastery will work in concert with the desire of God for sons to move towards inheritance. Inheritance is always the desired result for all seasons of sonship. Those seasons for review are: Invitation, Interdependence, Interchange, Invocation, and Inheritance.

5- TRANSPARENCY

Trust issues within sonship work against healthy transparency being communicated to fathering leaders. Transparency, when healthy, is life-giving. However, there is a risk within this area of sonship submission because as long as the son desires things out of context to purpose, he or she could lose a fathering leader's buy-in. As discussed within salesman sons, as long as the son has an end-game in mind, the fathering leader must resist until that end-game is consistent with purpose. Transparency should increase throughout the movement of each season of sonship, and like all areas of sonship, submission must be intentional.

If the son is firmly established upon the pillar of perspective and releasing honor to a fathering leader who is receiving revelation to lead the son, why is transparency required? The answer is simple but deeply revealing. Transparency is more for the son than the fathering leader. Many times, a fathering leader has the revelation that is just now arriving in the life of the son. **The fathering leader may be watching to measure trust as revealed within transparency to ensure the process can be finished, not just started.**

I have fought the good fight, I have finished the race, I have kept the faith.
-2 Timothy 4:7

Fathering leadership is after developing finishers. Jesus, as a fathering leader, emphasized His finishing as if it was the prime positioning of purpose. His entire earthly life and ministry were aimed at finishing well. Fathers are not interested in starting even though sons often wish that grander celebrations would be held when something new was started. Pomp and circumstance don't a mature son make. Fathers are after finishing, sustaining, and enduring. Transparency is a gauge of what trust level the father has with the son.

The father needs to know if the son has the trust level that will become required for finishing the process that transparency often begins. Even if the son believes the trust is adequate, the fathering leader will look to the blueprints of purpose made available within the fathering perspective to know if the process can be sustained to the finish. Sons desperately need many finishing victories within sonship. As long as there is a quitter within the son, the son is not ready to inherit.

Communication

Transparency is not only about information flow; the process of being transparent is healthy to involve God in all parts of the communication process. As the son opens up to the father, trust is gained in the son as the fathering leader's responses more accurately reflect Jesus than previous leaders or natural fathers. This is powerfully true when sons have been in abusive situations that celebrated performance. Fathering leaders often look deep within the motivations of communication to understand how influences are impacting a son's soul health.

For the word of God is alive and active. Sharper than any double-edged sword, it penetrates even to dividing soul and spirit, joints and marrow; it judges the thoughts and attitudes of the heart.
-Hebrews 4:12

The process of communication within transparency allows the sword of the spirit to begin to lay open places within the heart that have come to the surface in transparent communication. This is not to cause hesitation in the son, but clarity on how deeply involved God desires to be in the very marrow of the thoughts, the place of thought production at the motive level, the place where the Holy

Spirit can lead into all truth. When fathering leaders capture, by discernment, areas that remain unhealed that are giving life to thought processes, emotional cycles, fears, or overreactions, and healing can arrive through a son posturing himself, greater trust in Fathering leadership and God abounds all the more.

For this reason, transparent communication should be an intentional sonship discipline. When areas arise where the son is mature, he will realize when he desires to withhold transparency, and that becomes telling. Holy Spirit is ready to respond on why there is hesitation in this transparency. Where transparency abounds, fantasy dissolves. This is because if an area of pride (which is deception) is communicated to a leader, the fathering leader can determine whether the son is in a position to deal with the issue or if further trust is required. The fathering leader can intervene or extend mercy for a time.

As will be discussed in timing, just because the son has communicated something and won the battle of transparency, it does not mean that the time to take action has arrived, or that the son can leverage the fathering leader outside of the proper timing. The fathering leader has learned the lesson of timing, and through these experiences, so will the son. In sonship, ignorance is not always bliss, and anger that comes from the feeling of being ignored can be quite revealing of attitudes within the heart and unhealthy fathering expectation.

Throughout the processes, within the protocols, and around the promises of sonship, there will be times where hidden things remain hidden from the son and even the fathering leader. Just as repentance and confession are different in that one is saying something and the other doing something, the fact that a son is ready to ponder something within himself does not necessarily indicate he is ready for the ramifications of change. Transparency can signal readiness to a fathering leader.

When the discipline of transparent communication is fully grasped, written communication is sufficient for fathering leadership function no matter the distance. It was true in Paul's leadership to Timothy, Titus, and other sons' lives and remains true today with the availability of technology, which makes fathering leadership more scalable than ever before. While immature sons continue to demand proximity, mature sons learn the process that makes proximity a luxury more than a necessity thereby exchanging quality over quantity. Because of the leadership of Holy Spirit making available all that is desired and empowering, the distance between father and son is not an issue when transparent communication is the burden of a mature son.

Practically, this is accountability via reporting. A transparent email can open up a yearlong process of sonship progression that encapsulates training, inner healing, deliverance and discipling — all of this comes from transparent communication. Furthermore, this can and has happened when the fathering leader assigned by God has had little verbal or written response to the email. This is because, again, Jesus is thoroughly involved in the release of all things required for the relationship's purpose to be manifested.

Often, God, through a revelation of Holy Spirit, will honor the process by speaking things that bring the same result in the son had he heard them out of the mouth of their fathering leader. This process does not limit heavenly father, Jesus, and Holy Spirit involvement in the life of the son. That involvement becomes exponentially more experienced.

As the son honors the father, God can and does move mightily to fill in any place of natural weakness or unavailability so that the result remains the same, ensuring God gets what He desires no matter the spiritual fathering leader's weaknesses, as long as He is the one that defined the relationship.

The Little Yes

Although spiritual sons across the world have gotten away with giving God the "big yes" that resulted in little obedience, fathering leaders are looking for the consistent and repeated "little yes" that becomes markers of sonship submission. This will grow a son's submission to the level that they are no longer are willing to say "No" to God in any area, no matter how small or seemingly insignificant. The world is not won with the big yes, it is won by the little ones that require follow through.

Many missionaries accepted the call to the nations. However, a fathering leader can examine that same leader unable to pay their bills. The missionary desires to go to the nations and live in the dirt, and yet that big yes to them has covered all of their weaknesses in their mind which are apparent to those around them. While religion would cheer and allow that person to do whatever they desire as long as it didn't push the status quo, fathering leaders will not allow that person to misrepresent Jesus with personal lives that were never impacted by a big yes.

The fathering leader says, "Take a class on finances"; the missionary says, "No." That one "no" just negated the big yes made directly to God in the day of passionate response. "Who will go for me," echoes throughout the heart of every missionary, yet most missionaries today burn out with marriages that fail, kids that prodigal, and lives that end in bitter waste. The big yes to God that does not result in repeated little yeses within the process to reach purpose, results in an understood no. Fathering leaders will not let that fly as they will test the yes!

Strength From Outside

Transparency clarifies areas that the individuals believe are areas they have said yes, are actually, areas where they are "living" the opposite. Fathering leaders will be able to see this, and work to provide leadership. The individual has not had enough personal leadership to make the necessary changes required to end that type of cycle that could result in failure, so, the fathering leader can exert leadership to the level of trust and deal with those within the right timing.

Transparency with a fathering leader trains sons and daughters to get real with God and to be intellectually honest with themselves. This kind of posture produces submission which gives way to rest and peace. I have had this happen in my own life in many ways, one which sticks out. I was in the place of questioning God's motive towards me. I had helped other's escape the orphan spirit yet there were places within me still untouched by the spirit of adoption. I decided to get real with God, mostly because hiding had not done much good.

I remember distinctly saying, "Lord I have gone all over the world for you, been in nations, preached the gospel, seen miracles, people giving their lives to you powerfully, and yet here I am in this mess." His response came through crystal clear and hit me like a ton of bricks. Looking back, I can correlate directly how my fathering leader had prepared me to hear truth by maturing me to the place of loving correction. The Lord spoke, "Most of what you did was run and try to escape the place of your pain that came through the neglect of your natural father."

My motives were instantly laid bare right before me. I was secure enough in that moment to weep. I had been lying to myself for many years. My motive was to run, and my call to nations had become the greatest escape. The call of God had become an avoidance of pain. I never had to keep a job, steward relationships well or finish anything, because, in my mind, the day would come where I would have to sell everything and move half-way across the world. I figured the best way was to go ahead and not have anything to begin with. I was deceived.

Not everyone can hear the Lord that way. Many people, including some great prophetic leaders I have met, always hear words of positivity from the mouth of God, and never correction. They instantly assume fathering leaders who bring correction are from the devil. They filter the voice of God through their feelings towards themselves, many times with their religious prayer time making them feel so happy that they always assume God is happy. Days didn't set me up for that moment; years did. As the testing of that time continued, fathering leadership helped me endure and pass each one.

Trust Empowers Transparency, And Transparency Enables Trust

The seventy-two returned with joy and said, "Lord, even the demons submit to us in your name." He replied, "I saw Satan fall like lightning from heaven. I have given you authority to trample on snakes and scorpions and to overcome all the power of the enemy; nothing will harm you. However, do not rejoice that the spirits submit to you, but rejoice that your names are written in heaven."
-Luke 10:17-20

Transparency within fathering leadership from a son produces the opportunity to let go of claims to himself. This is vastly important in a disciple of Jesus' lifestyle. When a son declares Jesus as Lord, he removes the claims to himself. Practically, in modern Christianity, many still have claims to things, people, money, jobs, themselves, and other areas where the yes has not yet penetrated.

As a son progresses through the seasons of sonship, revelation and favor will increase. As the increase comes, transparent communication will provide the opportunity for maturity in understanding what arrives. It comes because of kingdom citizenry; being born from above awakens magnificent sights and sounds as will be discussed in the Season of Invitation. All celebration is anchored in adoption as Jesus makes clear to His disciples, however, leadership means mastery.

Transparency empowers teaching moments with a fathering leader. As the trust grows, transparency should grow. What is an intentional discipline at first becomes a flow that releases excellent power. As your leader gains your trust, grant him your transparency. If a leader demands transparency, that is controlling, but if a son offers transparency via accountability, it will produce great fruit and further accelerate the progression of sonship stature. Healthy transparency with my fathering leader has never hurt me in the past ten years, but it has helped me more times than I can count. It empowers a communication flow such that even when interaction is low, the impact is high. A "yes," with oil is better than a thousand words.

6 TRAINING

You, however, know all about my teaching, my way of life, my purpose, faith, patience, love, endurance, persecutions, sufferings—what kinds of things happened to me in Antioch, Iconium and Lystra, the persecutions I endured. Yet the Lord rescued me from all of them. In fact, everyone who wants to live a godly life in Christ Jesus will be persecuted, while evildoers and impostors will go from bad to worse, deceiving and being deceived. But as for you, continue in what you have learned and have become convinced of, because you know those from whom you learned it, and how from infancy you have known the Holy Scriptures, which are able to make you wise for salvation through faith in Christ Jesus. All Scripture is God-breathed and is useful for teaching, rebuking, correcting and training in righteousness, so that the servant of God may be thoroughly equipped for every good work.
-2 Timothy 3:10-17

This is an insightful passage to understand Paul and Timothy's fathering relationship. Timothy didn't only know Paul's teachings, but he knew them thoroughly. Timothy would have read Paul's books had he wrote them. Timothy didn't only understand Paul's victories, but his suffering. Timothy was allowed to realize things in Paul's life, not just because they were friends, but because these things produced opportunities for Timothy to be trained. By being part of Paul's life, Timothy had victory available from battles he never fought. Paul granted him access.

Timothy was around the scriptures from a young age, but Paul's fathering leadership transparency brought Timothy directly into the deep levels of training where those scriptures could be applied through him and not just to him. Although this will be more discussed in the <u>Season of Interdependence,</u> Paul walking with Timothy through experiences prepared Timothy to be ready for them when they arrived in his life. This is a vast difference between fathering and other discipling strategies.

Think back to the pillar of perspective. The son must remember that the assigned fathering leader sees at a different level, more aware of purpose and less interested in potential. From this revelation, the leader can lead. This perspective is what makes him the leader to begin with! From this place, (and the fact that the fathering leader has gone through the seasons of sonship gaining experience and expertise), training opportunities are completely consistent purpose are produced.

Training: Potential vs. Purpose

It is easy for those who are coming out of other subcultures to quickly misunderstand training based upon potential versus training based upon purpose. The risk is that the son who has invested 30 years into potential-based training or self-help might see the purpose-based training pathway before him as "waste" because it ignores potential completely. Some of the training may have been close enough to potential to be useful for the son to progress to purpose, but it cannot shorten or alleviate purpose-based training if it has no eternal value.

Grace is released to empower purpose-based training. This is why part of the father's passion will burn against obstacles that hinder the flow of grace. As Paul ran "the course set before him," it is easy to see that course was set by another. He was separated to that purpose in Acts 13 and running the path to that purpose was his life. This was not a sprint, it was an endurance marathon. Paul's crown was for completing that course, finishing the job hence, why He put it within His letter. Paul was not tooting his own horn, he was sharing this important fathering principle with a son he would later charge to teach it to others.

The Race Set Before You

The Fathering leader sets the course in preparation for the son. The fathering leader knows by revelation, experience, and expertise what part of that training is consistent with the purpose and what can be ignored. This is why fathering all children in the same fashion is a mistake. Just as all "natural" children are unique, "spiritual" children are unique also and require their fashioning to be customized. As sons progress into greater stature within seasons of sonship, training may change. This training is not just sharpening gifts, but ensuring the proper character is in place to finish well.

Discipleship programs without a fathering heart cannot be the end-all. Discipleship without a fathering heart that is marketed to the masses will provide some benefit as teaching can occur with biblical values, but without leaders that have a father's heart, that program alone will not progress sons to maturity as heirs. The same is true with Bible Schools, Seminaries, Pastoral training, and other healthy aspects of Christian instruction. Without fathering reaching the heart, the orphan that is allowed to exist within the spiritual son will limit all of those. Fathering leadership is more effective at dealing with deep levels that limit the son than other methods.

Fathering leadership allows God to be more involved with His children in meaningfully transformative ways. It doesn't mean that sons will never get outside training, but their father can be involved at some level even if that level is awareness. A father may not tell a son called to carpentry to take a class on electricity but would be able to assist the son in gathering any fragments of knowledge that could be useful from it, for example.

With my spiritual fathering leader, I have understood his training involvement in 5 different ways throughout the last ten years.

Five Levels Of Training Involvement

Avoidance- The fathering leader believes the training should be avoided for one or multiple reasons. If the son struggles with previous abuse, the fathering leader may have to work to try and communicate in a way where the son still feels in control. If the fathering leader thinks the training will be harmful no matter how the son may respond, he will speak up.

Awareness- The son has made the fathering leader aware of his desire to train in a particular area. The immature son will sign up, pay, and then inform their fathering leader of the decision he made. If this happens, the fathering leader will often work after-the-fact to see how the training can be fit within the blueprint of purpose, if at all. The mature son will run by the fathering leader to see if the training is consistent with how they understand their purpose. This way, waste of time and resources inconsistent with purpose is avoided.

Acknowledgment- The fathering leader acknowledges the training is not a bad idea but doesn't have a lot of insight into how it fits but realizes it may. He leaves a lot of liberty for the son to pursue as desired.

Agreement- The revelation of the training arrives to the son. The fathering leader agrees that the son should commence with the training as it does fit into some sense of the blueprint of purpose.

Admonishment- The training opportunity arrives through the fathering leader who is involved in some way or is struck with the feeling from the Lord that the training is directly connected and urgently needed for the son to undergo. This is the level where Fathering leaders often lead their sons in training. This level of training connects "urgent" and "unction."

Remember that fathering leaders are not controlling leaders and do not desire to make all the decisions for their sons and daughters. If you have a leader who is controlling, they are not functioning as a father. This doesn't mean that the fathering leader cannot be stern, and they should be. A firm answer is essential in some issues, while others can take a lighter feel. Often times, the leader's correction can be measured based upon the son's maturity. Sons easily bent are lightly corrected and adjust accordingly. Stubborn sons often take a firmer hand in the areas of training.

Ready Before You're Ready

Dr. Don Lynch says, "People think they are ready before they are ready." This is a true statement. In my experience, I have realized that, often times, I think I am ready to do something but when it arrives it leaves me tested and winded. Having had multiple experiences in this area, I learned to settle and trust in the training pathway that has been given to me through my fathering leader. I am faithful to it.

The constant nagging, "Is it over," questioning is more like a servant waiting to be paid, than a son being made ready to inherit. The finish line for each training phase is not always based upon measurements the son can identify. Sometimes, the son requires one more lap to realize in the training, that there is more within him than he realizes. Training pushes sons to realize there is something within them they have missed or vastly underestimated.

Fathers are Pace Setting Leaders

I allow my fathering leader to be my pace setter in the preparation, and am accountable and transparent as I walk through it, so that anything I miss can be discussed. This has become easier for me as I have no other desire, I can discern, outside of seeing God glorified. My father has walked me through being set free from the delusional fantasies of glamourous ministry through access he has granted to real ministry, real time.

I have also learned to not try and get out of the training early. As will be discussed as part of timing, my fathering leader is more qualified than I to tell me when I have finished. It is too easy to stop before things are finished, and even more importantly to learn that since sustaining is so essential, to the purposes of God, endurance is always required in every aspect of training.

This intentionality has helped to mature me more rapidly. After traveling together, hundreds of emails, thousands of text characters, ministering together, serving together, and preaching his material before my own, I can tell you that submitting to your fathering leader's training will be of great benefit to you and the sons and daughters who come after you. Like my fathering leader says, "You think you are getting ready to hold your Isaac, but really you are being prepared to offer your Isaac."

The difference in how you start and how you finish each stage of training is directly related to your maturity as a son, and if you can carry fruit from the training forward into the next stage you have success.

7 TESTING

The heart is deceitful above all things
and beyond cure.
Who can understand it? -Jeremiah 17:9

The areas of sonship submission are areas that, by mastery, will enhance, expand, and accelerate the progression of sonship stature. The greatest fathering leaders in our generation will be those that master these areas. The last two areas of sonship submission increase in intensity as the son progresses from the seasons of preparation and moves into the seasons of positioning. Tests are mile markers that often exist within the transition of one season to another. A son cannot carry forward and wield a weapon when a test hasn't proven its usefulness in their hand.

This is one of the ways to understand a son thoroughly equipped as one who has a tested weapon that can be carried into battle. The fathering leader can use a tested son as a weapon within the shared assignment, and that son, as he masters weapons, will carry them into more significant battles. Much of sonship is having successes in growing battles. A defeat that occurs in the seasons of sonship can be a victory, if the son is positioned correctly and can learn from the experience to carry that maturity forward. The biggest battles lay ahead for the son, the greatest exploits are his future!

The way in which a son interacts with testing changes through each season of sonship. In the earliest stages, testing, the idea, the process, and the experience go under-appreciated. Testing, by design, is not meant to be the most enjoyable aspect of the sonship experience. If testing isn't difficult, it isn't testing. Each test should reveal something not deeply known before the testing began. Often, what is revealed in testing provides guidance as to what areas exist within the heart that may still be immature. This will get God's attention, and should get yours, as the enemy will capitalize on any area of immaturity.

The Heart Of A Son

Testing shows that there is more within the heart than the son realizes. The son can never know everything within his own heart, but either can the spiritual father. The chambers within the spiritual heart have many hidden areas that the Holy Spirit will desire to explore. The same spirit that knows God's heart knows the heart of a father and son. By revelation, the fathering leader's process can bring sons and daughters into strategic times where testing brings forth things previously unknown for both to work through together.

God gives tests to show the son there is more in him than he realized. This is not always about evil lurking in the heart but can also be about the greatness that lives there. Testing is the place to mature what is hidden so it can be manifested as a marker for maturity. While immature sons desire to avoid testing, mature sons realize that it presents a high reference point for the path and typically can only interact with it correctly because a fathering leader has taught the son how to embrace each test in order to overcome it. Fathering leaders know and understand testing.

For I wrote you out of great distress and anguish of heart and with many tears, not to grieve you but to let you know the depth of my love for you. If anyone has caused grief, he has not so much grieved me as he has grieved all of you to some extent—not to put it too severely. 6 The punishment inflicted on him by the majority is sufficient. Now instead, you ought to forgive and comfort him, so that he will not be overwhelmed by excessive sorrow. I urge you, therefore, to reaffirm your love for him. Another reason I wrote you was to see if you would stand the test and be obedient in everything.
-2 Corinthians 2:4-9

Paul marries love, and testing here, and yet the current generation feels those things should be divorced. Perhaps, this is why there is such a perverted sense of love rampant in the body of Christ? Paul has a fathering obligation to the Corinthian church to test and ensure that their level of obedience is full. Fathering leaders' roles are representative in testing as they are in all others. Becoming a place of deepened trust, these strategic leaders are used by God in three strategic ways I have identified during testing times.

Stabilize- See the target

Fathering leaders stabilize sons within times of testing. The intensity of the testing begins to make many issues within the heart surface. At times, this can be so intense, the son may miss the fact that a test has been issued. The fathering leader can help to explain what aspects of the test are legitimate, and what places are not, within the context of that testing. This clarity will assist in the son's endurance so he will not be distracted by improper prioritization.

Surround – Staying on target

The fathering leader can work to assist the son in not becoming a target during testing. Since hell is after the son maturing towards heirship, testing is a vulnerable time where the adversary can attack the son. While some of the attacks may be tied to testing, some attack is overly opportunistic and illegal for that time. The fathering leader, at times, has the perspective to understand what is in bounds and out of bounds for that particular time of testing.

Steady- Hit the target

Fathering leaders that have helped to identify the target will help steady the son emotionally to strike it. By instilling keen wisdom during testing, the son will realize that a higher perspective in sonship increases the chances of hitting the target without multiple failed attempts. Each miss is an opportunity for instruction and greater skill. The fathering leader is not after getting the test over with as much as developing skill before and during the test. During this time, issues that diminish the son's accuracy are becoming apparent, and as those limitations arise, they can be extinguished.

Letting go

Paul encourages in 1 Thessalonians 5 that prophecy be tested. He does this so that as prophecy is active in the body and is encouraged, those receiving should examine each prophecy so anything that comes out inconsistent with God's nature can be dismissed. Anything that is good or is consistent with who God is and what He gives can be received. Testing does this. It brings clarity to inconsistent areas that need to be surrendered.

This is like bringing thoughts into captivity to see if they are consistent with God, who He is, and what He gives, which is the knowledge and wisdom of God revealed in Christ. Some thoughts that are inconsistent with who God is, as revealed in Jesus, come up in times of testing. If testing is hurried, that pattern of thinking can go unchallenged. If a new pattern of thinking survives the test, it is proven and can be carried forward.

If a financial test brings up the feeling like God is not a good provider, it is an opportunity for repentance and greater revelation of the nature of God depicted within scripture. The victory that comes through enduring the testing and overcoming is increased authority in that particular area. It will become useful later when that newfound faith is tested particularly when the need is more prominent and more is on the line. The fathering leader wants to ensure when that moment comes, the son doesn't fail!

Three Ways To Flourish Within The Test

1) Allow the goodness of God to be an anchor, and gratitude, the chain that ties you to it. God tests from a place of goodness, not a place of evil. He doesn't desire failure or take any enjoyment in frustration. Often, the testing can be as hard for the fathering leader to watch as it is the son to endure. Where the testing comes from is extremely important. If testing makes a son feel as if God isn't good to them, it is showing a critical place where the son needs healing.

71

That kind of place could disqualify the son when walking in the place of destiny fulfillment.

I recall a place of testing within my life that showed me many things within my own heart. It centered around residue within me that the goodness of God was aimed at anyone but me. My daughter, who is now ten, had just been born. The financial crisis of 2008 had hit, and I lost a job at a large bank and was painting homes and doing odd jobs to survive. On top of that, my daughter had just been born eight weeks early. My wife had lost much blood during the emergency surgery and almost died. Now we were on our way home after a two-week stay in intensive care, and on top of all that, I didn't have money to purchase the specialty formula my daughter required.

I was fighting feelings of being defeated. My soul was in real anguish. Out of learned discipline, I would lift my voice in praise for the little miracle that God had given us, but the enemy would continue to arrive with accusation to steal any joy I mustered up. I was in the car pulling into the driveway, trying to figure out how to take care of our new baby until I could get the money to feed the family. As we pulled in late at night, I opened the mailbox by the driveway only to find that the mail that arrived that day contained a 30-day sample of the specialty formula we needed for our baby girl to eat. We wept, and our gratitude, even to this day, ties us to the anchor of God's goodness.

2) Have people around you that can encourage you in the testing and avoid those would permit you to get out of it before it is over. Certain times of testing have brought a period of certain influencing friendships in my life. My destiny is worth too much to God, my spiritual father, and me for me to not be intentional about relationships. The wrong kind of person around you in testing will give you permission to quit, half-step, or flat out rebel. The right kind of person will encourage you to endure the testing, to expand your authority, and take the narrow road.

These types of relationships become those who can "purpose pollinate" and not "obedience eliminate" in your daily testing. I have seen so many sons and daughters prodigal after a period where they were not intentional about the relationships they held close and those they ended. It may sound harsh, but Jesus makes it clear that anything that competes with His love in our lives shows us about how we truly feel about Him. A few years ago, a "spiritual sibling" within the ministry began to carry dishonor towards our shared fathering leader, I knew the relationship would have to be redefined.

Even though it hurt, I could not allow their dishonor to work against the honor that I carried toward my leader. If I allowed my honor to diminish, I would not fill up the treasury, so less would be available for me. Some said I was harsh, but time proved my steps to separate from that dishonor proved to be a significant step in personal leadership. The person that was validating the enemy's accusation, and ended up showing forth their true rebel nature, and refused to surrender to the Lord. The right relationships will help you pass the right tests.

3) Be intentional about pressing into personal devotion. No matter how great an influence your fathering leader has, his devotion is not yours. He cannot love God for you. He cannot carry the grace you need for your race. You have to seek the Lord during times of testing. Though, at times, during testing, His voice is absent, you must press in to deepen the well within your spirit. Too many sons fail because they don't know that God is their true Father.

You cannot go on the coattails of your fathering leader, and mistake service to your fathering assignment as the only personal devotion to the Lord required. Serving your fathering leader's assignment will expand your capacity for the anointing, but only Holy Spirit will fill the new void with Himself as you seek intimate times in the secret with Him. Sons who do not practice personal devotion can become fathers who only know the God of their yesterday, serving days old manna to only those gullible enough to eat it.

Sons should be tested. Sons should grow even to welcome the opportunity testing affords. As trust in this area grows, fathering leadership can dig in and deal with some of the most significant limiting factors for the son to progress in the seasons of sonship and become a mature heir of God who can receive an inheritance that can be expanded. These sons who do not shrink back will become some of the most significant representatives in these days.

8 TIMING

Several years ago, during the throws of testing, the enemy was working overtime to separate my family from our assigned fathering leader. I remember distinctly going before the Lord in a time of prayer and fasting, seeking the face of the Lord. What compounded the intensity of this time was the fact that other peer-level leaders were giving me a reason to doubt the word of my spiritual father and, to some degree, because of trust that had been previously established over a long period, I was falling victim to listening. I knew I had to hear from God again.

I checked my heart to ensure that I was not offended which can often cause sons to question timing. I was merely curious about what was in store for the next season of my life since I had been told I may need a new fathering leader for what was next. After several days of fasting and prayer, I heard the voice of the Lord come to me while meditating on the Psalms. Like a whisper, I heard within my heart that I was to give the next five years of my life to my fathering leader and our assignment without questioning it, no matter what. The "without question" was the part where God got my attention the most. These people were having me question things I previously held onto as truth.

The commitment simply permitted me to ignore little things that caused me to question my assignment. It was as if that commitment alone closed the book on the accuser's methods. When the questions like, "Maybe he doesn't care about you doing that," would come up, the answer was always the same. I would take the question captive with a short, "It doesn't matter; I have a word from God," rebuttal. This taught me to go after the Lord without distraction, and it empowered my pursuit.

As the five years ended, I was no longer asking the questions because the heart motive that was the source to those questions was healed throughout the process. I committed myself to another five years without questioning, and by the time that period was ending, I didn't even understand things the same way. What had started the process no longer even existed. I was a new man by the time my commitment was fulfilled.

Timing is tricky. I know many sons who can accurately discern timing in others but entirely miss it inside of their process. I know many sons who can serve great wisdom and revelation to others but miss it working in their own lives. For this reason, many of them are not yet fathering leaders. Their fathering leader is working so they are not a living discrepancy, ministering to others what they have failed to surrender. This is part of understanding timing within sonship and how it works.

Place Timing In The Hands Of Your Fathering Leader

This is one of the most straightforward areas of a son's submission decision. Sons should, upon arrival with a fathering leader, surrender the timing of their sonship process. It makes sense that sons cannot possibly move accurately within timing since they are unaware of the full picture that is purposefully hidden.

Most times, sons are not fully aware of what they are being prepared for. By surrendering timing, they are once again, allowing a higher level of submission to impact them. The nagging question of, "Am I ready, am I ready," drains more life out than puts life in. The fathering leader will ask, "Ready for what?" Normally, the son has no response.

Timing is critical, and as the seasons move from preparation in invitation, interdependence, and into the interchange, to the positioning seasons of invocation and inheritance, the son has matured in the understanding of the timing of the Lord. This, however, doesn't mean the son has perfected the patient endurance fathers have already mastered. Sons tend to be in a hurry when fathers refuse to rush. This implies a son may get ahead of their preparedness if they manage their timing. Time Management

Within the preparation seasons, timing usually feels adverse to sons. In the invitation, the infant thinks he is an heir, confident he can chew with no teeth. He begins to move out based on his handle of revelation, finding that what he felt was a worldwide word was meant to be a teaching moment between he and God that needed to follow a long prophetic process. Rather than receiving correction, because he has not yet grown to love it, he runs from it.

The process would have matured the son from the invitation to interdependence where he would have come to realize his need of a fathering leader not to be a "one-word wonder," but so that he could be the man who could walk within that word. This is why this area of sonship submission is so important and how it impacts the son's willingness for transparency. As the son's transparency increases and submission to his fathering leader's understanding of his timing increases, his maturity will increase.

The disciples commonly missed the aspects of timing, as it was beyond them spiritually. Their wrong handle on timing made them misunderstand the motives of Jesus-their-fathering-leader on several occasions. They assumed that Jesus knew all aspects of timing, but even within His leadership, He had surrendered His understanding of timing to the Father. Timing is always surrendered up, and that is the case to this day where Jesus is unaware of the time of His return.

Preparation and Positioning

Not having timing within their control is to a son's advantage because it is humbling and requires the fathering leader to receive a handle of it by revelation, and it keeps the son from being able to prepare and position themselves. Sons cannot prepare or position themselves, and if they do, they prepare and position themselves for the wrong thing and end up wasting all they have received. The son who won't let the fathering leader do his job of preparing and positioning is choosing a stranger and will end up eating with pigs.

Even as the son returned home in the story of the prodigal, the son could not position himself. All the son could do (because of the humility he learned through the process) was go to the lowest level possible and allow the father to position him differently. That process would have provided greater trust that would have continually grown. At each moment of timing change, if the son resists and misses it, it will hurt and not help.

Lifted Up

Humble yourselves, therefore, under God's mighty hand, that he may lift you up in due time. -1 Peter 5:6

Some sons so resist the fathering leader and their handle on timing that they struggle against the fathering leader being a representative of God lifting them up. They would rather God lift them in such a way that they appear to be the only person in the story. This is just not the correct way in which God will do this. Within fathering leadership expressed in sonship, when God promotes, the fathering leader is involved.

Some sons don't understand readiness in timing. They think when the fathering leader wants to focus in on a greater stature within a son, that perhaps they are not ready for that permission and need to continue in their current role or function. This may sound noble, but this resistance to the hand of the Lord is a subtle pride that puts the son's lifting on pause.

On the one hand, the healthy maturing son hears through the fathering leader that it is time for their stature to increase visibly, and it confirms something within them they have already been feeling but couldn't quite articulate. This son, even when subtle doubts arise, knows that if their fathering leader that God has assigned them says they are ready, they are ready. This is a Peter "at your word" moment. Peter asked Jesus to call to him so he could do the impossible because He was looking at those words to release the ability for the impossible.

Other immature sons, march to their own drum right out of time. Instead of being part of the formation, they end up being a one-man-show. They feel something is being held back that they are ready for before they are ready. They are ready for the first step in many cases, but not the fifteenth. Their bad handle on timing sets them up for missing the moment. Sons like this, need to rest in their submission, until they can understand the times and seasons of the Lord.

Conclusion

We as sons are always looking for the key of timing in the mouths of our leader. If God puts a word on time in their mouths, we expect God to honor His word and make grace available to do that feat no matter how radical or impossible it seems. This doesn't always mean it will work out as we feel it should. It does say that we believe that what God has brought together, no man can tear asunder! This covenantal reality works within fathering.

Allow yourself to experience the surprise and embrace the mystery that can unfold within an authentic and healthy fathering relationship. As you stand on the pillar of pursuit, the wind of God will blow you into places prepared before you long ago. As the pillar of posture is mastered, God will lift you up at the right time, in the right way, and into the right place. As you are secured in the pillar of purpose, all distractions will teeter and fall like sticks blown into the fire that doesn't go out. As you walk upon the pillar of perspective, you will learn to embrace the mysteries of heaven, and the reality of your spiritual inheritance will cascade down like waterfalls from the throne.

As you submit to your fathering leader, being transparent, you will find areas come unlocked that he or she can help push open. Your testing moments will be cheered on by a great cloud of witnesses as your promotions arrive, within the timing of the Lord. As you train with your fathering leader for a race you do not yet fully understand, you will increase in endurance. It is required to run the race that may take your lifetime, but finding yourself faithful at the end of it, you will honestly find yourself more than a conqueror, as you were always destined to be. With this end in mind, let us begin.

That person is like a tree planted by streams of water,
which yields its fruit in season
and whose leaf does not wither—
whatever they do prospers.
Psalm 1:3

To be continued in…
Seasons of Sonship, The Season of Invitation.

ABOUT THE AUTHOR

Joshua Todd is happily married to his wife Coral of 12 years with two beautiful children. Todd serves with Dr. Don Lynch, of Ministry Matrix International & FreedomHouse, A Kingdom Center in Jacksonville Florida. As the Academic Dean of Students with Kingdom Leadership Institute, Todd is part of an expanding global initiative that touched 24 nations in 2018 with international leadership. As an author and speaker, Todd is faithful to function in an Apostolic Call with a Prophetic anointing. Todd received his Master's of Practical Ministry in 2016 and is preparing to receive his Doctorate. To contact Joshua Todd about more information, you may contact him at joshuaftodd@gmail.com.

Manufactured by Amazon.ca
Bolton, ON